Praise for
Matthew Paul Turner and
OUR GREAT BIG
AMERICAN GOD

"Matthew Paul Turner has written a fascinating biography of God—specifically God's sojourn in America. This book is enlightening, funny, and filled with so many historical insights, I found myself uttering 'Aha!' at least twice per page."

—A. J. Jacobs, *New York Times* bestselling author of *The Year of Living Biblically*

"OUR GREAT BIG AMERICAN GOD by Matthew Paul Turner combines history, social commentary, and good writing into a powerful work that tells us just why we Americans are all so crazy—*God made us do it!* If you want to understand America, read this book."

—Frank Schaeffer, author of *And God Said, "Billy!"*

"A delightful overview of American church history with a perfect blend of sarcasm, irreverence, and love. Illuminating, engaging, and playful, this book is the best thing that has happened to America's God since, well, America. You will love this book, provided you're not a Calvinist."

—Ed Cyzewski, author of *The Good News of Revelation* and *A Christian Survival Guide*

"Whip-smart, wry, acerbic, and surprisingly tender, OUR GREAT BIG AMERICAN GOD is a grand family tree of the union between God and America. As a Canadian who is often baffled by—while still very influenced by—this great big American God, I found Turner's book enlightening, bold, and downright funny."   —Sarah Bessey, author of *Jesus Feminist*

"I read Matthew Paul Turner's books for two reasons: he's been a good friend for years and his ideas always challenge me. The question, 'Who have I made God out to be?' is a critical one to wrestle with, and this book provides the gym for the match."
        —Jon Acuff, *New York Times* bestselling author of *Start*

"In this book, Matthew Paul Turner gives us a glimpse into how the church in America has been trying its best to destroy Christianity, and gives us some hope that it might just survive regardless."   —Peter Rollins

"With humor and refreshing candor, Turner has once again challenged the status quo, dared us to all to challenge our preconceived notions of God, and succeeded in bringing our eyes back to a God that just simply loves us all."
                —Timothy Kurek, bestselling author of
                                The Cross in the Closet

"Who knew I could have this much fun reading about Puritans, Great Awakenings, and Jerry Falwell? Who knew a historical book about American Christianity could make me laugh out loud and still cringe at my own hypocrisy? Matthew Paul Turner's story of America's God may make you uncomfortable. It may even offend you. But you will walk away from this book wiser. You will long to know a God outside of culture and time, a God unmarked by humanity's stain."
        —Micha Boyett, author of *Found: A Story of Questions,*
                                Grace, and Everyday Prayer

"The pages are packed full of history, but Turner's approachable and cheeky writing style make it truly entertaining. It's funny, provocative, and exceptionally well written. A must-read."
—Nish Weiseth, author of *Speak: How Your Story Can Change the World*, editor-in-chief of deeperstory.com

OUR GREAT BIG

American

GOD

A SHORT HISTORY OF OUR
EVER-GROWING DEITY

MATTHEW PAUL TURNER

JERICHO
BOOKS ™

New York Boston Nashville

Some people's names and identifying details have been changed to protect their privacy.

Also, I've elected to use the masculine pronoun for God, not because I think that God possesses a gender, but for the sake of narrative flow and because all of the people I write about in this book refer to God using male pronouns.

Unless otherwise indicated, Scripture quotations are taken from the King James Version of the Bible.

Jericho Books
Hachette Book Group
237 Park Avenue
New York, NY 10017

www.jerichobooks.com

This author is represented by Daniel Literary Group.

Printed in the United States of America

RRD-C

First Edition: August 2014

10 9 8 7 6 5 4 3 2 1

Jericho Books is an imprint of Hachette Book Group, Inc.
The Jericho Books name and logo are trademarks of Hachette Book Group, Inc.

The Hachette Speakers Bureau provides a wide range of authors for speaking events. To find out more, go to www.HachetteSpeakersBureau.com or call (866) 376-6591.

The publisher is not responsible for websites (or their content) that are not owned by the publisher.

Library of Congress Cataloging-in-Publication Data has been applied for.

For Jessica

CONTENTS

OUR GREAT BIG

American

GOD

PROLOGUE

Where would God be without America? My friend Dave asked me that question a few years ago. I thought it was an odd query, but by the look on Dave's face, it was also a serious one. Dave and I had been engaging in a mostly friendly debate about whether or not America was a "Christian nation"—I said, "No," and he said, "But it should be"—when, right in the middle of a back-and-forth about the role that the religious doctrines of the Puritans played in helping to shape American culture, he blurted out his question in an obnoxious "I gotcha" tone. Staring at me like we'd suddenly entered the inquisition part of our conversation, Dave smirked. "It's not a complicated question, Matthew."

A few moments later, I shrugged. "I guess I don't know the answer. Tell me. Where would God be without America?"

"I have no idea. Which is my point. Without the United States, God would probably be a tourist attraction in London or maybe homeless in Canada." Dave thought for a second. "Or buried in a secret library in the Vatican's basement." My friend grinned, but only long enough to take a breath. "What I'm trying to say is that America has been very good to God. And I'm convinced that God wouldn't be nearly as popular today without this country."

"Are you suggesting that God needs America?"

"Not exactly. But I think he's better off with us than without us."

To prove his point about God's semi-dependency on America, Dave rattled off a nine-digit number and told me that was how many copies of the Bible that America had distributed around the world in the last ten years. He listed off the names of fifteen or so white evangelists—"good godly men," he said—and then told me that no other group had produced more "born-again decisions for Jesus," here and abroad, than American Christians. Dave mentioned the number of American missionaries, the number and variety of American Christian radio stations, how many times in a year Americans plant new churches, and a larger-than-I-expected dollar amount for how many American-written Christian books had been sold the year before. And then, hands flapping, Dave talked about our nation's love of Christian stuff, our passion for helping people in other countries find freedom, democracy, and Jesus, and our eagerness for keeping prayer and other Christian values in the cultural spotlight.

Blazing with enthusiasm, Dave said, "Do you see what I mean, Matthew? We've helped to make God famous and known throughout the world. What other country has even done half as much as the United States in promoting God?"

The longer Dave talked, the more he made God sound like an American tourist attraction, a family-friendly exhibit, or a ride at Dollywood suitable for kids who were more than forty-two inches tall. He made God sound like a brand name, one proudly made in the USA.

When Dave finished telling me all the reasons why he believed God needed America, I said, "Well, I don't think anybody questions the fact that America and Christianity have shared the same bed from time to time. But I hate to break it to you, man, God gets around. So suggesting that God needs us in order to remain famous and relevant seems like a stretch. I mean, you've said a lot about America. But you're making God sound like a deity who's in the fetal position in the corner of a room rocking back and forth."

I could tell that Dave was becoming restless with our conversation, so rather than pressing my point further, I decided to blurt out an uncomfortable question of my own. "So is it true?" I said. "Have you really joined a Christian Zionist movement?"

Suddenly, Dave's interest in talking to me was resurrected. He reached into his briefcase, pulled out a three-fold pamphlet, and pointed to what looked like a hand-drawn picture of Israel. "It all comes back to this tiny piece of land right here, man. It's all about God's people."

Having grown up in a small nondenominational church, Dave told me he'd learned early on about God's love for Israel, but never thought about how it impacts Israel today. Eventually, Dave's telling me about his journey toward embracing Christian Zionism brought the conversation back to where our talk began: Was the United States a Christian nation?

"America isn't God's chosen country," he said, "but right now we are God's most important country when it comes to aiding the affairs of Israel." He tapped his fingers on the map. "It all comes back to Israel. That's been God's plan all along. Since America's beginning. Since Abraham, really. God loves America, but we're just a means to an end."

He meant *the* End, as in the final minutes of the Eleventh Hour, the Last of the Last Days, that moment in the Book of Revelation when the Divine Fat Lady brings down the house, so to speak.

Dave talked about the End like a child talking about the Magic Kingdom, full of wonder and delight. "I don't fear what's coming," he said. "I'm looking forward to it. And I actually get to be a part of it."

Dave told me that the End was a foregone conclusion, that there was nothing we could do to stop it from happening, that God's final initiative was already set in motion. "It could happen at any time." In fact, according to him, the only unanswered question is how we as America's Christians help the process along. And that's where the Christian Zionists come in.

"We are actively looking for ways to help God with his conclusion. That's what we believe is our calling, our mission, what God wants from us."

"Please tell me you're joking, Dave."

"Joking? Of course not. I would never joke about something like this."

I was speechless.

"Dave," I said. "How exactly does somebody help God with the End?"

My question made Dave uncomfortable. Eventually I was able to get him to disclose that one of the ways the members of his home church were helping "the cause" was by funding an organization that encourages (and pays for) young Jewish-American professionals to move to Israel. He explained that by helping Jews "return to their homeland"—the homeland most of them have never visited, mind you—they fulfill biblical prophecy about Israel becoming whole again. Dave and company were also working through a comprehensive biblical prophecy study, a video course led by Chuck Missler, a biblical futurist who lends his scriptural knowledge to uncovering secrets about what the End will bring. He, along with his wife, Nancy, also runs a Christian Zionist mission called Koinonia House. At the time, I'd never heard of Missler and figured he was just some fringe apologist who had a cult following online. But I assumed wrong. Missler's following is large, spirited, and apparently includes Robert Downey Jr., who once mentioned his love for Missler on Jon Stewart's *Daily Show*.

"Listen, man," Dave said, "I know you think I've turned into a nutcase. But eventually, God's truth will be revealed. And perhaps then you'll understand."

"I'm sure I will. Brimstone is rarely confusing."

"Don't joke about this, Matthew." A half-cocked grin cracked across his face. "If you study your Bible, you'll see that everything I'm talking about is there in black and white. And despite what you might think, God is not your punch line, friend."

"We live in America, Dave. People here have been making God into a punch line since the beginning. I'm not suggesting that's a good thing, but it's true nonetheless. We Americans have attempted to create and shape God's narrative for centuries."

Dave rolled his eyes and started gathering his belongings. After packing his Bible, notebook, and highlighter into a backpack, he swung it across one shoulder.

"But when you're living God's narrative, how can that be a bad thing? The fact remains that no other country has done more for God than America. We are a part of his story. And while we aren't perfect, we are—"

"A means to an end. You said that already. Just remember, Dave, the scariest punch lines involving God always come from people who aren't joking. We both know that."

Dave stood up. He turned around, forced a smile, and said, "And Matthew, you know as well as I do that punch lines are only scary for those who aren't in on the joke. That's why we keep sharing the joke. Right? So we can get as many people in on the joke as possible. Because we know for a fact that whosoever isn't in on the joke will not like the punch line."

"Are we still talking about God, Dave?"

He didn't answer. I'm not sure he could answer that question, at least not honestly. The more we talked, the more I began to think that Dave was still getting to know his most recent concept of God, still learning God's dynamics—how he/she/it

5

worked—and how he fit in. But Dave's divine story wasn't simply one that he was reading and discovering; by all indications he believed that God's was a story he was helping to write, shape, and manipulate. Not only that, but he'd cast himself as a participant in the narrative, not a major character, perhaps, but somebody whose actions affected the outcome of others in the story of God.

He's not alone. To some extent, we are all "growing" God, stuffing his mouth full with ideas, themes, and theologies, fattening him up with a story line we believe to be true. Our intentions may be good, but then again, I'm not sure intentions matter when it comes to God's image. For good or bad, we are all molding God to reflect our own personal, American interpretation of Christian faith.

. . .

For four hundred years, America has been "God's Country." At some point after the death of Queen Elizabeth I in 1603, and before the formation of the Massachusetts Bay Colony in 1629, a group of religious outsiders from Great Britain decided that God needed to cut his losses in theologically wrecked Europe and start fresh in the newly discovered western hemisphere. What transpired is a relationship between deity and geographical location like none other.

While "God's Country" isn't exactly a divinely inspired moniker, we can't deny that God is one of this country's favorite pastimes, an almighty part of our Americana, like playing baseball, cruising strip mall parking lots, and popping antidepressants. Americans love God so much that he's threaded throughout our national history, printed in all caps on our national currency, combined with patriotism and embroidered onto hats and polos, and inked with needles into the bodies of a multitude of American hipsters. God happens a lot in this country. Why? Because America has always welcomed God with open arms, congressional protection, free speech, and tax-exempt status. And even though laws have been created to define how, where, when, and to what extent God is allowed to happen in America, with a permit or two we can pretty much do whatever the hell we want to with God, just as long as somebody cleans up his /our mess. Regardless of how one defines our relationship to God, whether you see it as an on-again, off-again affair or a holy matrimony, one thing is clear: God and America have been exchanging DNA since the beginning.

According to Gallup, nine in ten of us answer "yes" when asked whether or not we believe in God. That's down from the 1940s, but only slightly. And while atheism and agnosticism are on the rise, and there are more Americans identifying as "nones"—nonreligious people—than ever before, God is alive and well in America.[1] But who is America's God? It's true that the word "God" is rather ambiguous, often meaning different things to different people. Believing in God in America can vary from believing in Jehovah, Jesus, or Allah to believing in Nature, a "Spirit Mother," or some other grand Universal presence that usually enjoys silence and book clubs. Today, one person's God is another person's fairy princess. Still, the majority of Americans believe in God as defined by Judaism, Islam, or Christianity. And not surprising, 77 percent of us identify "God" in the context of the Christian faith.[2] This book is about that God, the one in which three-quarters of us believe. But that statistic begs repeating my earlier question: Who is this God of American Christianity? Is it the God who is worshiped by congregations that belong to the Presbyterian Church of America? Or is it the God who is worshiped at congregations that belong to the Presbyterian Church (USA)? Is the Assemblies of God's God America's real God? Or is God a Baptist, and if so, which kind of

Baptist: Southern, Primitive, Free Will, Old Regular, Reformed, Independent Fundamental, Sovereign Grace?

Is God Methodist? A Lutheran? A Nazarene?

An Episcopalian?

Did Jerry Falwell, the preacher and political pundit who founded Liberty University, once worship the same God that pastor and *Purpose Driven Life* author Rick Warren currently worships? And is Rick Warren's God comfortable sitting in the same room as the God whom Pentecostal evangelist, healer, and magician Benny Hinn worships? Can the God of American Christianity be both the God of the Quakers and the God who is worshiped by gun-fanatical evangelicals? Is God pro-life or pro-choice, pro–birth control or pro–natural family planning, pro-war or pro-peace, pro-Israel or pro-Palestine, pro-gay or pro-straight? Does God have a gender? Does God favor men over women? Or does God believe in equality?

Even when defined within the theological, political, and social boundaries of American Christianity, there's a wide range of ideological possibilities for "God"—"Creator of the Universe," "Greek Orthodox," "God hates fags," "universal salvation," and everything from believing that sinners are held in the hands of an angry God to believing that God occasionally abducts small children and takes them on exclusive guided tours of heaven. Are the ways of God predetermined? Or is God, when interacting with humanity, more of a Great Observer than a Holy Meddler?

America is affecting God. While that idea goes against the orthodoxy that America's mainline Christian churches adhere to—that God is the same yesterday, today, and forever—still, can we truly deny the fact that America's God is not the same as America's God was in the beginning? The United States of America affecting God isn't a new occurrence. Since our country's conception, the men and women who conceived of our country's ideas and values also helped create a fertile environment for God to change and shift, grow and evolve while oddly remaining the same in our eyes.

Today, among those of us adhering to American Christianity, "God" is a very adaptable word, a vernacular ice-cream cone that we accessorize, decorate, and smother in something decadently sweet. Many of us, after topping our God with our ideals of what he represents—hope, politics, marriage legislation, worship songs, or a literal hell—invite others to taste and see that our God is good. Because most of us believe, regardless of what we've piled atop our two scoops of God, that he—our American God—is good.

. . .

This is not only a book about God, it is also about God's people, more specifically, God's *American* people. In the process of writing this book, researching and collecting stories, immersing myself in this country's history, and refamiliarizing myself with the beliefs, ideas, and passions that Americans embrace about God, I was reminded how closely related people are to the story of God. It is the one constant regarding the history of religion; the worship of anything is as much about humanity as it is about the God or god(s) that people worship. In some cases, that's all it is about.

Most of us learned about God's story through the stories of Abraham, Moses, King David, and the Prophet Daniel. While God played an important role in the plotlines of each of those biblical narratives, was God the most important character? Maybe. For many, the supernatural parts of biblical narrative are the themes that might spark our imagination to wrestle and wonder about the divine, but would we even give the "unbelievable" a second thought if the story offered no humanity in which to relate? I doubt it. Frederick Buechner said that if you dig beneath the surface of a person's theology, you'll eventually find their personal story. Buechner's 1970 book *The Alphabet of Grace* started with these words: "At its heart most theology, like most fiction, is essentially autobiography." He continues, mentioning the names of theologians like Aquinas and Tillich, "[These men are] working out their systems in their own ways and in their own language, are all telling us the stories of their lives, and if you press them far enough, even at their most cerebral and forbidding, you find an experience of flesh and blood."

My New Testament professor once put me in my place regarding God's role in our story. "Mr. Turner," he said in a tired voice after a long debate, "people are always involved in God's story. Even when we're not the subjects, we're always the narrators."

For four hundred years, Americans have narrated God's story, and during that time, God has grown and evolved, become bigger and more unbelievable. Our stories have added theologies and folklore, miracles and fear, pro-*this* narratives and anti-*that* themes, ghost stories and strobe lights, Sarah Palin and more than a little humanistic sensibilities. In our efforts to make God known, we've quite possibly turned God into something that resembles us, a big fat American with an ever-growing appetite for more. What follows is the story of God as told, shaped, and affected by America. Because God is not the same as he was yesterday, not here, not among America's faithful.

CHAPTER ONE

AN AMERICAN RESURRECTION OF GOD

In 1801, a rumor spread across the United States that God was doing something miraculous in the tiniest of places, Cane Ridge, Kentucky. According to James Bradley Finley, a then nineteen-year-old from North Carolina, the rumor was true: A mighty work of God was happening, a spiritual revival like nothing he'd seen before.

"The noise was like the roar of Niagara," Finley wrote later in his autobiography. This wasn't far-fetched, considering twenty-five thousand campers had congregated on that field in the middle of Kentucky and there were reports of people being "tossed to and fro" by the Spirit of God. Finley described God as "like the tumultuous waves of the sea in a storm" and the crowd as "like the trees of the forest under the blast of [a] wild tornado." For five days, Finley watched God do things he'd never witnessed before. A longtime Presbyterian, Finley was uncomfortable with what he saw, at least in the beginning. But the young conservative Christian warmed up to the experience, eventually calling it a "most astonishing and powerful revival," the biggest movement of God since "the day of Pentecost."[1]

America's Pentecost happened during the first week of August in 1801, when God brought together the largest group of people that most of the attendees had ever witnessed first-hand. The majority were Methodists, Baptists, or Presbyterians. Considering that Methodists stood on the opposite end of the theological spectrum from Presbyterians, and that most Baptists stood wherever their pastors told them to, their willingness to worship together was a marvelous achievement, perhaps the most miraculous part of what happened at Cane Ridge.

Denominational unity was for the most part frowned upon by a majority of America's churches. Still, like Finley, those who attended God's party in the Bluegrass State weren't accustomed to *seeing* God show up, let alone seeing God show up carrying a bag of heavenly tricks. Finley wrote about people becoming "struck with terror and conviction, hastening through the crowd to escape, or pulling away from their relations, others trembling, weeping, crying for mercy, some falling and swooning away." Finley said that God moved through the crowd like a tsunami, slowly engulfing people in the Spirit, causing people to hop around like pogo sticks or to perform backflips off wagons and tree stumps. Amid the chaos, God, according to Finley, stirred up "a universal cry for mercy, [a] bursting forth in loud ejaculations of prayer or thanksgiving." This work of the Holy Spirit, Finley admitted, "exhibited nothing to the spectator...but a scene of confusion."[2]

Then, amid all of that divinely inspired ejaculating, God also killed a man. That's how Finley tells it, that God killed "a daring blasphemer," a pompous blowhard who, upon becoming drunk with liquor, stupidity, and the devil, mounted his horse and started riding straight through circled gatherings of prayer. After interrupting two or three prayer circles, "[the man] fell from his horse...as if hit by lightning." Finley watched as a multitude of people gathered around the man's lifeless body, cheering and shouting "as if Lucifer himself had fallen."[3] Too interested in what he witnessed, Finley "watched [Lucifer] closely, while for thirty hours he lay, to all human appearance, dead." The following day, the man's lifeless form began twitching and shaking. Leaping from the ground, he hopped, skipped, and performed somersaults while shouting nonsensical sounds of pleasure and praise. These temporary murders happened quite often according to Barton Stone, one of the ministers who preached at Cane Ridge, who said that "the falling exercise was very common among all classes, the saints and sinners of every age and of every grade, from the philosopher to the clown. [They] would generally, with a piercing scream, fall like a log on the floor, earth, or mud, and appear as dead."[4]

Behold, the strange works of God in America were at hand in Cane Ridge, Kentucky, in 1801. Whatever happened that week, whether every detail written by the people who experienced those Spirit-filled days is true, false, or somewhere in between, the truth is that the larger-than-life camp meeting altered the future of God. How could it not? The God that the men and women experienced on Kentucky's hillsides was one that most Americans had never before encountered. In the months and years following "America's Pentecost," spirit-filled revivals broke out across the nation, causing a multitude of Americans to become entranced in holy bliss, overwhelmed and intoxicated with the Spirit of God.

America's God had indeed grown since his Puritans days, days of piety when wigs and robes were worn behind pulpits, and few things were more exciting than catching one's neighbor living a secret life as a Baptist or, worse, an Anglican. Could the God who was causing people to get down on all fours or lie slain in the spirit really be the same God who led the Puritans across the Atlantic from England to Boston? And if so, what on earth happened in America to cause such a shift in how people experienced and worshiped God?

Whatever it was that happened to God between 1630 and

1801, the transformation continued after the revival in Cane Ridge. If America's God was indeed the same yesterday, today, and forever, then it would seem that God's understanding of "same" was evolving.

. . .

In the spring of 1630, the story of God was on the brink of change, a new beginning that would forever affect how humanity interacted with the divine. According to John Winthrop, one of the men in charge of organizing the initial stages of God's transition to the New World, a fresh start was all a part of God's dream for America. God had big plans for Winthrop, or maybe it was the other way around. Either way, this quiet but feisty Puritan lawyer was elected governor of the Massachusetts Bay Company, a position he was well suited for, considering Puritanism fit him like a straitjacket. Early on, Winthrop wasn't a big proponent of organizing a mass exodus out of the Church of England, but eventually he became convinced that not only did the Puritans need to leave Great Britain, but God wanted him to play the role of white European Moses and lead God's people out of the Old World.

Winthrop imagined himself as a Puritan of biblical proportion, and believed that "Operation New England" was about far more than he and his buddies having more space to stretch their spiritual legs. "Thus stands the cause between God and us," Winthrop wrote in his thesis, "A Model of Christian Charity," a personal declaration of sorts that boasted Winthrop's vision for what America might become. "We are entered into covenant with [God] for this work." The work that Winthrop alluded to was no small task, either. The New World's Moses was convinced that he and his fellow Puritans had been divinely called to create a utopia, a Promised Land where God and his people would prosper. "We shall be as a city upon a hill," he wrote, "[and] the eyes of all people are upon us."[5]

The vision that Winthrop saw was that of a holy and magnificent existence, a spectacle so bright and lovely, it would cause people to stop, stare, and feel jealous that they weren't a part of it too. Though Winthrop hoped that the work he and his Puritans were about to engage in was going to change the course of history, little did he know that his actions would also alter the story of God.

. . .

In many ways, the term "Puritans" is misleading, because it implies that Winthrop and friends were one unified religious group. But in truth, these "radical Protestants" consisted of people from many different religious factions. They didn't necessarily agree on all theological points. Their "unified" name, "the Puritans," was given to them because of their common desire to purge the Church of England of what they considered to be unbiblical religion, which included anything that smelled like pope. When they failed to purify England's church of Catholic traditions (the Roman Catholic Church was a religious institution that many Puritans called the Whore of Babylon), these disgruntled Protestants began conspiring to move God to a new and mostly untainted continent far, far away from the loose churches of England and Rome.

What were the Puritans thinking, bringing God to a New World? By most accounts, their leaders were quite intelligent people, many of them educated men and women with a dutiful love for God. So did they really think that moving God to an untamed wilderness was the best alternative, particularly for *their* God: a sovereign, doctrinally stout, damnation-prone deity who despised change and hated the sight of human skin? It's no secret that the Puritans' God wasn't the easiest to get along with. He was stuffy. And finicky. And sometimes barbecued heretics.

The God of the Puritans was basically the same God that John Calvin had encountered almost a century earlier. Like Martin Luther, Calvin believed that the Roman Catholic Church was vile, and he became a vocal and influential supporter of the Protestant Reformation. However, amid his war against Catholicism, Calvin also developed a new spin on God, a spiritual thinking about faith, sin, and Christianity that emphasized the doctrines of God's sovereignty, predestination, limited atonement, and the supreme authority of the holy scriptures. Calvin's God was big, in control, and at times choosy about whom he held hands with. One hundred years later, among the Puritans, John Calvin's God had also evolved to become nitpicky, hellbent on human holiness, and impossible to please.

Still, the Puritans dedicated their lives to making God happy. Which wasn't easy, considering they viewed themselves as a depraved group of people, hideous and rotten to their very core. The Puritans saw themselves as ill-minded refuse whose souls were filled with cobwebs, demons, and nasty fixations for deviant pleasures. They were Calvinistic in their thinking there as well. Somewhere along Calvin's spiritual journey, the angst-prone priest became convinced that God thought humans were disgusting creations, dirty little beasts whose filth began in their bowels, which dumped into their souls. "Total depravity" became one of Calvin's most affecting theological tenets. Essentially he had refashioned Saint Augustine's theology of "original sin," the idea that Adam and Eve's sin in the Garden of Eden was so great that sin became genetic, an unholy gene that preconditioned every human born after them for sinful behavior. Calvin took it a step further. From his perspective, humans were not just genetically predetermined for sin, they were evil beyond repair, and in fact incapable of doing the slightest "good" in the eyes of God.

Considering their God was so hard to please, it's a bit surprising that nobody pondered how their plans to move him to the New World might make him feel. This was the early 1600s, remember, and God had only recently started engaging in quasi-personal relationships with some of England's common folk. This new idea—God hanging out with regular people—was primarily the result of the availability of the 1611 King James Bible. Still, God's availability to the common man was limited at best. Most people couldn't afford to purchase God's Word, and even if they could, the chances that they could read and understand it were dim. Until this time, engagement with God happened in communities, at churches, and by way of pastors and priests telling people what God thought about them. The Puritans certainly had visions of making God more accessible to people without the need for bishops and priests, but as it were, their God was just beginning to learn how to teach middle-class people with moderate comprehension skills about the depravity of their own souls. If their God only had minimal experience with everyday English folk, how comfortable was he going to feel developing relationships with indigenous people whose genitalia he might see?

Truthfully, moving God probably wasn't their best option; however, from Winthrop's perspective, it was their only alternative. But since not all of the Puritans agreed, Winthrop knew that convincing those still on the fence about moving would be strenuous. So when it came to framing the big move into a narrative, one that might make the adventure seem exciting and divinely inspired, Winthrop went to the one thing that Puritans almost always relied on when it came to framing big scary unimaginable ideas: He used theology. Theology was the fairy dust in the Puritans' kingdom, the magic potion for motivating a company of fear-filled people to step out in faith and do something brave, difficult, and incredibly stupid. Even among today's American Christians, theology is still a pretty convincing manipulator, mostly because it's often guilt-inducing. And few things motivate conservative Christians more than a holy helping of guilt poured atop a Bible verse taken out of context. Our "fairy dust" today is far less rich and smothered with scripture than what the Puritans offered. Contextual integrity as it relates to the Bible wasn't something the Puritans often considered when applying biblical narrative to everyday circumstances or enormous adventures that might kill you. Winthrop and company didn't worry about things like context; they were far too preoccupied with their journey's subtext: Run away from the Whore!

So shortly before Winthrop was set to depart with an undetermined number of people for greener (and Native American–inhabited) pastures, the Reverend John Cotton traveled to the port of Southampton, England, carrying with him an important message. Reverend Cotton's gracing the future travelers with his presence was a big deal. Not only was he one of the most respected clergymen in all of the Church of England, but he was by all accounts the most important Puritan voice in the entire country. Cotton represented the purest parts of the Anglican Church, and though at the time he wasn't planning to join the party in America (he would, in 1633, decide to move), his support was, according to Winthrop, heaven-sent.

And the message Cotton brought with him? It pretty much changed everything.

. . .

"Moreover I will appoint a place for my people Israel, and I will plant them, that they may dwell in a place of their own, and move no more." That's how the Reverend Cotton began his lecture to the Bay Colony, with a passage out of the Second Book of Samuel, a beautiful sentiment about God looking for real estate to plant a beautiful garden of Jewish people.

Like Winthrop, Cotton doesn't waste time considering the context of Bible verses; he's too focused on selling the big idea to worry about its truth. Cotton arrived at Southampton on a mission, to separate the chaff (the Euro-losers) from the wheat (the Future American Winners) and give these scared-out-of-their-minds men and women a reason to believe that moving twenty-seven hundred miles from everything they knew and loved was a fantastic idea. By the time Cotton finished, preaching about moving to New England wasn't just a grand idea, it was the greatest idea in the history of ideas. And most importantly, it was God's idea, one that he'd designed on their behalf before the foundations of the earth had been formed together.

Though Cotton's sermon was wordy beyond repair, he delivered one of his best theological conjurings on that day. Not only did he make the Children of Israel disappear from the narratives of a number of Old Testament stories, but he intentionally inserted a brand-new noun in the stories, replacing the people formally known as God's chosen people with God's new chosen people, the Puritans. By the time Cotton completed his sermon, he had stood with his Puritan brothers and sisters at the edge of the Jordan River and they had witnessed together their first sight of the Promised Americaland. He'd led them to the walls of Jericho (which looked a lot like Massachusetts) and marched before them until they all came tumbling down. He'd battled alongside them and killed Philistines, Moabites, and Native Americans. He'd braved with them the brute strength of a British Goliath and sent Great Britain's fleets, cannons, and redcoats hightailing it back to the Old World. Using chapter and verse and a whole lot of theological imagination, the great John Cotton put his soon-to-be colonists squarely in the middle of God's biblical story, weaving together with words a holy narrative, a marvelous adventure of Puritanical proportions, a miraculous destiny where God's new chosen people would become the recipients of God's providence, God's promises, and eventually God's executive order to do whatever the hell they wanted. God's vision seemed almost too good to be true. But not according to Cotton.

Standing before a packed house at the Church of Holy Rood in Southampton, Cotton inspired the attendees' minds and hearts with a collection of words he called "God's Promise to His Plantation."

"I will plant them." Cotton spoke that sentiment four different times to the future colonists, a way of describing God as an Almighty Gardener. Cotton told his spiritual brothers and sisters that the Good and Gracious Gardener was preparing to plant a mighty forest in the New World. He said that God's Puritanical garden was going to be huge, far bigger and more lush than any of his previous gardens, and that they should not be filled with worry, because the Gardener would be sure to care for his little seedlings, that they should find comfort in the fact that God would till, weed, fertilize, and water them regularly. But there was more. If everything went as planned, if the Puritans were well behaved and followed God's commands, the Gardener would grow the New World's forest into mighty "trees of righteousness."[6]

Adding to the God-vision, Cotton said, "When he promised to plant a people, their days shall be as the days of a Tree. As the Oak is said to be an hundred years in growing, and an hundred years in full strength, and an hundred years in decaying."[7]

On that day Cotton prophesied a major story line, not only for himself but for all of the Puritans. And while he presented it as God's plan for the Puritan people, it was more or less Cotton's Puritan plan for God. He ended his eighteen-page sermon with a mighty declaration from God Almighty:

For consolation to them that are planted by God in any place, that find rooting and establishing from God; this is a cause of much encouragement onto you, that what he hath planted he will maintain, every plantation his tight hand hath not planted shall be rooted up, but his own plantation shall prosper, & flourish. When he promiseth peace and safety, what enemy shall be able to make the promise of God of none effect? Neglect not walls, and bulwarks, and fortifications for your own defence; but ever let the Name of the Lord be your strong Tower; and the word of his Promise the Rock of your Refuge. His word that made heaven and earth will not fail, till heaven and earth be no more.[8]

Reverend Cotton changed the story that day. He single-handedly steered the course of God's future in the same direction that the Puritans were headed. No wonder the Puritans failed to consider how the New World—and soon-to-be United States of America—might affect God. Because in their minds, this big move became less about pursuing religious freedom and everything to do with following the divine destiny that God had called them to. What was that divine destiny? The Puritans believed that it was their responsibility to resurrect God from the dead, to fight tooth and nail to keep God safe and out of the hands and parishes of the Whore of England.

The truth of Cotton's words didn't matter. People believed they were true. Belief, under the right conditions, almost always trumps truth. And sometimes belief can manifest its own truth. Nevertheless, the Puritans did exactly as Cotton requested. They flocked like geese to New England. Over the next ten years (from 1630 to 1640), during what many historians call the Great Migration, more than twenty thousand Puritans made America their "Promise Land," their home.

And thus America became God's home too.

• • •

Not long after God, John Winthrop, and the rest of the Bay Company arrived on America's shorelines, the news from the Old World turned bleak. With every arriving ship, more bad tidings were reported. England's troubles in many ways caused the seeds of nationalism to gestate in the hearts and minds of the Puritans. These people had just traveled nearly three thousand miles to a new home. Considering that some arrived sick and others didn't arrive at all, many were thinking, "This was a mistake!" While it might seem dark and mean-spirited, even for Puritans, learning of the bad news happening in England—of Anglican officials becoming bigger bullies toward their Puritan brothers and sisters, sentencing many to prison, torture, or execution, and scattering others into hiding—revived many of the doubters' faith in their decision to make theirs and God's future in the New World. The Old World's bad news was for the Puritans Good News indeed. Though God hadn't started printing study Bibles for women and teenagers, and heavenly 401(k) plans wouldn't become a reality for another 350 years, all signs seemed to suggest that the Almighty's exit strategy out of England was well under way.

One Puritan who seemed certain that God was leaving England was Thomas Hooker, a respected clergyman still living there. In fact, Hooker became so depressed about the events happening in his homeland that amid one of his great mournings he wrote, "As sure as God is God, God is going from England." The minister knew this to be true because God delivered the news firsthand. "What if I should tell what God told me yesternight," he wrote, which was rhetorical, since that question ended with this statement, "that He would destroy England and lay it waste?" Eventually, Hooker escaped his homeland safely. After a short stint in the Netherlands, he made a beeline to New

England. Boston seemed to be his only recourse since, according to him, that was where God was safe-housing "his Noahs," a moniker that spoke more about the genocide he was predicting for all of the non-Noahs living it up in England:

> So glory is departed from England; for England has seen her best days, and the reward of sin is coming apace; for God is packing up of his gospel.... God begins to ship away his Noahs, which prophesied and foretold that destruction was near; and God makes account that New England shall be a refuge for his Noahs and his Lots, a rock and a shelter for his righteous ones to run unto; and those that were vexed to see the ungodly lives of the people in this wicked land, shall there be safe.[9]

Like the Reverend Cotton, Thomas Hooker framed his ideas using Old Testament names and themes, inserting himself and the people he loved into the good parts and those who disagreed with him into the not-so-good parts. Hooker wrote with a desperate tone. And yet even as he joined his fellow Noahs aboard the "Ark" in Boston, he seemed to hold out a small thread of hope for godforsaken England. "Oh, therefore my brethren," he wrote, "lay hold on God, and let Him not go out of your coasts. (He is going!) Look about you, I say, and stop Him at the town's end...farewell, or rather fare-ill, England!"

God had not been an American for five minutes and already somebody was making his sovereignty into a melo-dramatic off-Broadway show. But this shouldn't be surprising, really. Certainty as it relates to faith—something that the Puritans weren't in short supply of—always leads to exaggerated displays of religiosity. As most of us know, certainty makes us cranky, reactive, and always two prophetic signs away from "the End." Which was exactly how the Puritans viewed America, as God's last stand! America was the world's last hope, a grand fulfillment of Luther's Reformation, a second installment of the Israelites' Promised Land, and about as close as we were going to get to the divine fruition of the Kingdom of God. In other words, the City Upon a Hill just got skyscrapers and a subway.

. . .

That America would become God's shining example to the world of how society and religion should coexist has been a narrative threaded throughout our nation's history. John Winthrop's vision of a "city upon a hill" has become one of America's unofficial mottos. Though I doubt Winthrop intended his use of Jesus's words to become such an overused political tagline for speeches and op-ed pieces, that's just what happened. Derivatives have been used by American people in every arena, from preachers to politicians to pundits. Some people use the phrase to praise America's "Christian history." Others use it as a way of chiding the American people for trying to undermine Winthrop's dream. Most often, when Winthrop's "city upon a hill" gets mentioned, at least in a serious manner, it's for political effect. A host of U.S. presidents, from John Adams and Abraham Lincoln to John F. Kennedy and George W. Bush, have offered their unique spin on the sentiment. Even Sarah Palin paid homage to the phrasing during her run for vice president alongside Senator John McCain in 2008. In *America by Heart: Reflections on Family, Faith, and Flag*, Palin writes, "America is an exceptional nation, the shining city on a hill that Ronald Reagan believed it is." Palin combines Winthrop's ideal with an idea that many call American exceptionalism, a concept that paints America as the greatest nation in the world. Palin writes that "many people don't believe we have a special message for the world or a special mission to preserve our greatness for the betterment of not just ourselves but all of humanity."[10]

Ronald Reagan loved borrowing the words of Winthrop to define America, something he did throughout his political career. But in 1989, during his final speech as president, Reagan sat in the Oval Office and explained his own vision:

> The past few days when I've been at that window upstairs, I've thought a bit of the "shining city upon a hill." The phrase comes from John Winthrop, who wrote it to describe the America he imagined....He journeyed here on what today we'd call a little wooden boat; and like the other Pilgrims, he was looking for a home that would be free. I've spoken of the shining city all my political life, but I don't know if I ever quite communicated what I saw when I said it. But in my mind it was a tall, proud city built on rocks stronger than oceans, windswept, God-blessed, and teeming with people of all kinds living in harmony and peace; a city with free ports that hummed with commerce and creativity. And if there had to be city walls, the walls had doors and the doors were open to anyone with the will and the heart to get here. That's how I saw it, and see it still.[11]

Was that how John Winthrop saw it? It's not that Ronald Reagan's vision was particularly evil, but Reagan's "city" is very much a nationalized idea. Winthrop seemed far too consumed with the pursuit of humility[12] to cast such an American-focused ideal. As a Puritan, he certainly doused his "humble thoughts" with more than a dash of pride; still, he can't have imagined an America that resembled anything remotely similar to the Godtropolis that Reagan (and Palin) seemed to visualize.

Or perhaps Reagan was right. Maybe Winthrop's "city upon

a hill" was indeed a municipality brimming with capitalism, patriotism, and a very liberal immigration policy. Lucky for Reagan, Winthrop never fully explained the details of his vision.

However, two generations later, one Puritan did expound on Winthrop's "city." Cotton Mather, a Puritan preacher, had been inhaling American exceptionalism since he was a kid, an ideology he no doubt inherited from his father, Increase Mather, and his grandfather Richard Mather, both celebrated clergymen of the Bay Colony. Though Mather was born nearly three decades after Winthrop's death, his professional work showcases a lifelong interest in the Bay Colony's first governor. Not only did Mather write a two-part biography about Winthrop, but in 1710 he paid homage to Winthrop's "city" in *Theopolis Americana*, which means *God City: America*:

> Our glorious Lord will have [a] holy city in America, a city the streets whereof will be pure gold. We cannot imagine that the brave countries and gardens which fill the American hemisphere were made for nothing but a place of dragons. We may not imagine that when the kingdom of God is come and his will is done on earth as it is done in heaven—which we had never been taught to pray for if it must not one day be accomplished—a balancing half of the globe shall remain in the hands of the devil, who is then to be chained up from deceiving the nations.[13]

Cotton Mather had drunk the Kool-Aid, the juice made by John Cotton and John Winthrop seventy years earlier. Mather believed that God had created the universe and that front and center he had carved out a spot for America. Is Mather's *Theopolis* the America that Sarah Palin prays for, a holy city with streets made of gold and underground pipelines filled with black gold? An America that stomps around the world like she owns the place? Because at the heart of this kind of relationship between God and America—one that seems to believe an "executive order" is just another way of saying "thy kingdom come, thy will be done"—there sits a swelling amount of pride, a nationalized pride, a pride that continues today to shape our understanding of America as well as our understanding of America's God.

While the Bible says that pride goes before a fall, in America's case it also goes before a rise to power. And while we rarely hear people today brag like Sarah Palin does about how exceptional America is, the narrative she promotes still plays out in our country's Christianity, from the intent and purposes of our missionaries to how Christians in some areas of the United States treat Muslims to the powerful roles that Christians still play today in areas of politics, domestic affairs, and foreign policy. This American pride is found in the very roots of our nation's God, a God who would soon put America squarely in control of our own destiny. And perhaps by default, in control of the destiny of God.

CHAPTER TWO

THE TOTAL DEPRAVITY OF GOD

How did the Puritans' God become America's God? There were several ways, but the most influential was the Puritans' love for and dedication to Calvinism. Most of America's earliest stories about God are Calvinistic stories.

The Puritans were not the only people packing up their religions onto boats and sailing them across the Atlantic to the New World. But other sects didn't possess the Puritans' fortitude. God's new chosen people were an intense group, filled with a determination unmatched among America's earliest settlers. Many believe it was their deep dedication to their Calvinist faith that helped New England's transplants dominate early American institutions, from churches and public offices to high positions at seminaries and universities.[1] While it's impossible to know for certain, it's quite possible that America would not exist, at least not as a sovereign and free democracy, without the God-guided, man-enforced, rule-oriented theologies of John Calvin. As a study of God, Calvinism focuses on destiny (both transient and eternal), emphasizes glory (both divine and human), and stresses holiness (both spiritual and physical). No other Christian understanding at the time was so perfectly designed (by God, no doubt) for creating a civilization out of nothing.

The Puritans were also a driven people because of their great fear of hell. Nothing motivated hard work, good behavior, and a righteous need to serve the good of their community like a constant anxiety about whether or not God would send them to hell when they died. Their unease led some of them into massive bouts of depression, suicidal thoughts, and long, laborious sessions of prayer and confession. But among most, the thought of eternal damnation gave them a good reason to join the alliance and build a civilization.

Calvinism not only influenced how people thought about God in America, it also gave them the sense of moral obligation to fully embrace their personal roles in education, enterprise, infrastructure, or government to ensure that their "New World" became the success they dreamed it to be. Because from their vantage point they weren't simply building a Puritan society, they were building a society for God, an idea they were willing to fight to produce and fight to protect. And fight they did.

. . .

In February 2011, two weeks prior to the release of author Rob Bell's *New York Times* best seller *Love Wins*, a spiritual commentary about heaven and hell, Justin Taylor, a conservative Christian blogger and member of the Gospel Coalition, a consecrative conglomerate of bloggers who promote Reformed theology, watched the promotional trailer for Bell's book and wrote a post suggesting that the then head pastor at Mars Hill Bible Church in Grandville, Michigan, might be a universalist. To Taylor and his blogging cohorts, there are few things more useless, more dissenting, and more detrimental to their God's grace than universalism. Regarding Bell, Calvinist bloggers had been out on a witch hunt for years, seemingly obsessed with the preacher's beliefs, trying on various levels to put a noose around the pastor's theologies and let the Christian floor drop out from beneath him. So, having read only a short portion of *Love Wins*, Taylor wrote that "it is unspeakably sad when those called to be ministers of the Word distort the gospel and deceive the people of God with false doctrine."[2] Within a few minutes of Taylor's publishing the headline "Rob Bell: Universalist?," social media started buzzing with hellfire and brimstone toward Bell and his assumed ideas. After unleashing hell, Taylor updated his post with words from the Apostle Paul's second letter to the church at Corinth,[3] a holy, pleasing, and oh so passive-aggressive way of calling Bell a "servant of Satan" without actually calling Bell a *servant of Satan*.

But then John Piper hit the fan. The former pastor at Bethlehem Baptist Church in Minneapolis and founder of the online resource ministry Desiring God tweeted a link to Taylor's post with the message "Farewell Rob Bell." That tweet was Piper's cordial way of saying, "You're dead to us, Rob." That's what happens when God is left in the hands of angry people of faith. He becomes defensive when handled and shaped by our own self-importance. The big sovereign God that Christians usually boast about becomes a small and narrow-minded deity incapable of handling unorthodox ideas, at least not without humans helping him to carry the burden.

．　．　．

The only thing that might be more powerful than God is freedom. That was a lesson the Puritans would learn shortly after disembarking onto America's shores: that with freedom comes the ability to make personal choices, choices to believe or not believe in God, to adhere to one doctrine about God or embrace another doctrine altogether. Leaving these choices up to individuals was scary for America's first families. And the same can be said of many American Christians today. As much as Christians boast about freedom, many of us do so while not fully understanding its consequences.

One great misconception about the Puritans is that they fled to America in search of "religious freedom" in the broad, inclusive sense. That actually isn't true. Winthrop and company fled to New England in search of freedom to practice their personal religion. They wanted to create a place where they could worship God on their own terms, free from the Church of England's overbearing intrusion. They also had every intention of protecting their religion from anyone who might think differently about God than they did. True religious freedom would have required them to possess something of a tolerance for other religious ideas. But in truth the Puritans were looking for a man-run theocracy, a society they intended to keep righteous and unspoiled by any and all means necessary.

. . .

The Puritans' strong sense of faith, dedication to family, and close-knit communities sustained them during a myriad of circumstances, from providence to tragedy. Their confidence was found in the sovereignty of God—the belief that every single detail of their lives was under God's dominion. Most importantly, by submitting to God's authority, they believed wholeheartedly that every stroke of God's pen against the story of their lives was good. There was purpose in their pain, a divine thread within every tragedy. The death of a loved one? God had a plan. A mother who just suffered another miscarriage? A part of God's blueprint. An utter nuisance among the Puritan flock? Suddenly God's sovereignty was left in the hands of humans, either by democratic vote or totalitarian decision. Either way, living by God's sovereignty wasn't always pretty.

The Puritans adhered to God's supreme jurisdiction with such seriousness that it resulted in a grave case of self-importance. Which was one of the Puritans' greatest flaws; they were self-important to the nth degree, like a band of Martin Scorseses carrying Bibles, nooses, and dunking booths. Although their views on God and themselves inspired them to create a holy utopia, it also led to a superiority complex. Such a cultural frame of reference turned them into unreasonable people at times, especially when faced with dissension of those who lived among them. Any person who dared challenge the colony's understanding of God became an enemy not only to the well-being of God but also to that of their society. In other words, soon after they arrived, God turned into a controlling, state-run deity, the same God that had made England so impossible for them to endure.

The first to test the Puritan system was a feisty young minister named Roger Williams. Williams was known in the Old World for being rebellious and unorthodox. He was a Separatist (just like the Pilgrims of Thanksgiving fame who sailed to America's yonder shores in 1620), an early (and vocal) advocate for separating from the Church of England. Williams eventually fled England, and upon joining the Bay Colony he continued his knack for protesting the ruling religion's status quo. The worldly preacher soon became a thorn in the side of the Puritan leadership, and they grew weary of his constant critique.

Williams, however, would not be silenced. The travesties he witnessed while serving among the churches of New England were remarkably similar to the Church of England's sins. The Puritan churches were, according to Williams, acting like the Whores from the Old World. While pastoring a church in Salem, a congregation that was open to his more radical thinking, Williams preached that "all religious sects [have] the right to claim equal protection from the laws, and that the civil magistrates had no right to restrain the consciences of men or to interfere with their modes of worship or religious belief." Roger Williams despised church-sanctioned punishments—torture, jail sentences, and violence—against those whom church leaders deemed "heretics."

In many ways, Williams was preaching on his own behalf, as many among the Puritan elite called *him* a heretic. His offense? Williams believed that Boston should be a place of religious tolerance, a haven where people could freely worship God the way they chose. The religious leaders saw it differently: Williams was promoting "Satan's policy" by "[pleading] for an indefinite and boundless toleration." The Puritan ministers raged back, sneering at Williams's refusal to believe that the Bible demanded physical punishment and torture for those deemed "religious heretics." "[We are] the divine church order established in the wilderness."[4] That's how the leaders of Boston—the same ones who labeled Williams America's first rebel—defended their actions.

But Williams countered, "There was never civil state in the world that ever did or ever shall make good work of it, with a civil sword in spiritual matters." Though speaking utter Puritan, he basically said: *Oh yeah? That's bullshit.*

Retribution against Williams was harsh. "[Mr. Roger Williams] hath broached and divulged diverse new and dangerous opinions against the authority of magistrates . . . and churches . . . without retraction: it is therefore ordered that the same Mr. Williams shall depart out of this jurisdiction within six weeks . . . not to return any more without license from the court."[5]

In essence, that decree stated that God and the church had decided to cast Roger Williams out of the Puritanical Garden. The Puritans' shunning of Williams backfired in the end. Not only did the assumed "heretic" found Rhode Island, but his message of religious tolerance laid out a welcome mat for more people of various religions and creeds to find a home in New England. Soon the Puritans' God would be surrounded by the likes of Quakers and Baptists, and ironically, considering the Puritans had assumed their biblical identity, Jews. In 1644, Williams wrote and published a controversial defense of religious liberty, one that declared, "I acknowledge that to molest any person, Jew or Gentile, for either professing doctrine or practicing worship merely religious or spiritual is to persecute him."[6]

It's easy, nearly four hundred years removed from the Puritans' decision to banish Roger Williams, to decidedly judge them with our "evolved" worldview. Their actions toward poor Williams were, at the very least, un-Christlike (which really wasn't a Christian idea that the Puritans even thought about, especially in regard to *heretics*). That said, it is interesting the lengths the Puritans were willing to go in order to protect God from outsiders. The very notion seems to contradict their firm belief that God was an almighty, in-control, sovereign-beyond-all-biblical-reason deity. The Puritans weren't dreaming about "a more perfect union"; they were too busy building a most-perfect religion, following their own blueprint for the Kingdom of God, one seemingly void, at least in part, of the Beatitudes from the Gospel of Matthew, chapter five. But again, that's what made the Puritans so influential, because they were far too intentional to let God just be.

Safeguarding God against the ills of humanity was not simply the Puritans' desire; they believed it was their divine responsibility. However, rather than keeping God safe, their efforts created a stifling environment, a space that opened up opportunities for new ideas to arise and spread among their own people. They couldn't control people's beliefs. And the same is true today. As hard as we try to demand that God be this or declare that God hates that, in the end, our actions often undermine our understandings about the sovereignty of God. The Apostle Paul wrote that *if God be for us, who can be against us?*, his point being that God is with us and is powerful enough to take care of us. So if that is indeed true, and if we believe it, wouldn't God also be able to take care of himself? The obvious answer is yes. But then why do so many of us feel inclined to protect God against outside elements, both Christian ideas and non-Christian ones? America's Christians are defensive, known far more for what we protect God *from* than what we believe God able and willing to handle. Far too often our "sovereignty of God" suggests more about us than it does about God, a type of understanding that resembles spiritual individualism much more than it does faith.

. . .

The Puritans could not see their Christian discrepancies because they were much too busy putting out religious fires, ridding their ranks of heretics and ideas that threatened their theologies, traditions, and territories. Even as they were washing their hands of the Roger Williams mess, another problem was brewing inside the Bay Colony's camp. This problem's name was Anne Hutchinson.

According to John Winthrop, Hutchinson, a well-respected Puritan midwife who joined the Bay Colony in 1634, was dangerous. Over time, the colony's governor became convinced that Hutchinson was a cancer to the society he and his cronies had worked so hard to create. Writing in his journal, Winthrop described Hutchinson as "a woman of haughty and fierce carriage, of a nimble wit and active spirit, a very voluble tongue, more bold than a man."[7] Coming from Winthrop, none of those descriptions were compliments. However, as much as Winthrop disliked Hutchinson, there wasn't much he could do about her presence in the colony. For one thing, she hadn't done anything wrong. In fact, by all accounts, Hutchinson was a good, God-fearing Puritan woman who was well loved among the community. Perhaps the most threatening fact, for Winthrop anyway, was that she was well educated and able to match biblical wits with any man. That seemed to rub the governor the wrong way. "In understanding and judgment," he wrote, "[she's] inferior to many women, [and *again*] more bold than a man."

Why did Winthrop deem Ms. Hutchinson such a dangerous presence to the Puritans' survival? Because she claimed that God talked to her, and worse still, that he had given her a message. Historically, little is understood about Hutchinson's actual God experience, only that it happened while she was praying and the message she received brought into question the authority of the Puritans' church, doctrine, and leadership. Hutchinson's message from God contradicted the Puritans' beliefs about God. And according to Winthrop, that made her a threat to the colony's well-being.

Hearing God speak wasn't exactly unheard of among the Puritans. God certainly spoke to the Reverend John Cotton from time to time. Heck, the Reverend Thomas Hooker seemed to be in constant contact with the Almighty. But Hutchinson was a woman. At the time, God rarely spoke directly to women without a man being close by, so the very idea that Hutchinson had received a personal message from God was not only unusual, it was considered outright absurd. As Winthrop told her, hearing from God was "unfitting for [her] sex," but the fact that the message she received contradicted the Puritan belief system was spiritual treason, or as Winthrop put it, "[a transgression against] the laws of God and of the state."

The best part of this story, however, and the reason why it's important to America's narrative of God, is the actual message that God gave to Hutchinson. Much to the frustration of Winthrop's spiritual ego, Hutchinson insisted that God told her she was a member of the elect, or among those whom God would save from eternal damnation. As a result, Hutchinson declared two things: (1) that she could be certain of her eternal salvation, and (2) that she was no longer subject to the community's laws regarding outward appearance.

To Winthrop, it didn't matter what God had said, not when the message contradicted Puritan doctrine.

Puritans believed in predestination, a tenet of Reformed theology regarding salvation developed by John Calvin. Many Calvinists would argue that the Apostle Paul developed the concept, and therefore predestination was actually God's idea. Nevertheless, Calvin was the one who *developed* the concept, the idea that individuals are chosen by God before birth to either receive his gracious gift of eternal salvation or suffer eternal punishment in hell. In other words, Calvin believed that salvation wasn't for, as Jesus said, *whosoever*. According to the theologian, all of the "whosoevers" had already been chosen. Since God decided a person's eternal fate even before they exited the birth canal, it was determined that a person's salvation was a gift of grace, and could under no circumstances be earned by good works. Calvin described this "grace" as an irresistible gift from God, one that an individual could not escape. Yet this gift, according to Puritans, came with one horrific catch: Nobody was able to know for certain whether or not God had chosen them for an eternity of life or an eternity of damnation.

That catch is helpful if you're in the church business. But if you're hoping to develop a trusting relationship with a good, merciful, and loving God, it can be an almighty roadblock. For the Puritans, not knowing whether or not they were chosen by God led many to become OCD about acting and appearing as one of God's chosen. Heaven forbid somebody spend their entire life as a Puritan only to find out in the end that they were not on God's list. Leaders of the Puritan churches would gauge an individual's outward appearance as well as their church involvement and then declare them either (a) worthy to be a member of the community church and to take communion or (b) worthy of a good shunning. Being shunned was a big deal, because it meant you were a nonelect member of God's family and thus damned to hell. While John Calvin taught that God's grace was irresistible, the Puritans' grace was as confining as a prison cell.

With this in mind, imagine the sheer hell that broke loose when dear old Anne Hutchinson had the audacity to suggest God had told her that she was a member of the elect and furthermore above the doctrine of the Puritan church. In theory, Winthrop may have been able to overlook his personal discrepancies had Hutchinson kept her experiences with God to herself. But word soon got out that Hutchinson was not only having regular meet-ups with God, but she was telling other people about her holy infidelities. While aiding soon-to-be mothers with delivering babies, events that often brought large groups of women together in one house for long periods of time, Hutchinson began sharing her experiences and using scripture references to prove her point. Soon others began having personal encounters with God, and they too believed God had told them that they were among the elect and not subject to the church's bylaws.

The interest in Hutchinson's message among the Bay Colony residents grew so great that she began hosting Bible studies at her home, where sometimes as many as eighty people gathered. Hutchinson's willingness to share her God experience and hold unsanctioned meetings was bad enough. But perhaps her greatest crime was that she criticized the church's leadership, suggesting that God's men did not possess the Spirit of God.

Though Winthrop conspired to silence Hutchinson, she wasn't without influential supporters. In fact, the distinguished Reverend John Cotton, the very preacher who sent Winthrop and company off to the New World, was a chief proponent and mentor to Hutchinson in the beginning. He once wrote that in "her first coming she was well respected and esteemed. . . . I hear she did much good in our Town." But even the mighty Cotton couldn't squelch the fire that Winthrop would cast upon Hutchinson.

Eventually, Winthrop called Hutchinson to court, and, surrounded by deputies, officials, and a handful of clergy, there transpired a war of wit, words, and scripture memorization. The interaction between these two is a court transcript that reads like something written by Aaron Sorkin, almost too perfect, too concise, and too punchy to seem like a real dialogue. In part, Hutchinson's confidence, her strong sense of presence, speaks volumes to her character.

"I am called here to answer before you," she said, looking squarely at the eyes of her accuser, Winthrop, "but I hear no things laid to my charge."

Winthrop responded, "I have told you some already and more I can tell you."

"Name one, Sir," Hutchinson interjected.

That was how she handled every claim that Winthrop and his cohorts tossed her way, with short, confident answers. After reciting a list of charges and the punishment of those charges, one of the court officials asked Hutchinson how she knew her revelation came from the Spirit of God.

"How did Abraham know that it was God that bid him to offer his son?" asked Hutchinson.

"By an immediate voice," said the deputy governor.

"So to me by an immediate revelation," said Hutchinson.

Utterly confused, the deputy governor said, "How?"

The court officials, John Winthrop included, seemed befuddled by Hutchinson's faith, as if they didn't actually comprehend the relationship with God that she professed. The intimacy she shared with the divine seemed foreign, even heretical, to her accusers. And it became clear that the faith and trust she felt for

God was not the same as their own. Theirs was a relationship defined by knowledge and words, and hers was one she experienced and engaged. Interestingly enough, many evangelicals today would likely not consider people like John Winthrop and the Reverend John Cotton to be "born again," mostly because their relationship with God was a heavy-handed religion that paid no attention to Jesus or the Holy Spirit.

Toward the end of Hutchinson's court hearing, Winthrop's threats started irritating her. Her glare once again hit Winthrop between the eyes. "But now having seen [God who] is invisible I fear not what man can do unto me."

Winthrop's eyes widened. "Daniel was delivered by miracle; do you think you'll [be] delivered too?"

Hutchinson's response was brave, a statement that put all of her faith out on the table. "The same God that delivered Daniel out of the lion's den will also deliver [me]."

Unable to get a confession, Winthrop declared Hutchinson "delusional." All but three court officials verbally agreed. Winthrop announced to Hutchinson, "You are banished from out of our jurisdiction as being a woman not fit for our society, and are to be imprisoned till the court shall send you away."

People interpret the influence of Anne Hutchinson differently. Some see her as the first American feminist, confidently battling the ideas stacked against her by the men of her community. Whether or not she viewed Winthrop and his court officials as equals is unclear, but she did not view them as betters. And yet as easy as it is to view Hutchinson's strength as heroic, possibly containing a pro-feminist, anti–male establishment message in the subtext, the trial also cast a long dark shadow against the lives of many generations of women, particularly those in America's churches. In certain respects, Hutchinson's trial led to an increased silencing of women, not only in houses of worship but also in homes and communities. The word among the Puritans was that God judged Hutchinson for being a woman, a narrative that was spun to reflect her failure to *know her proper place.* Many Puritan ministers used her story to keep their churches in order and Puritan husbands used her story to keep their homes in line. Laced with fear, it was used to limit the influence that women had on men, on the church, and on the community.

Though Hutchinson was Puritan to a fault, she also showcased strength and faith that few Puritans, regardless of gender, possessed. Hutchinson's God wasn't the same God that the male-dominated Puritan church put their trust in. Her God was a personal God, a God that interacted with individuals. The truth is, Hutchinson's God was a far more American God than her accusers were used to dealing with. That's partly why they treated her so harshly. They did not understand her or her religious convictions. And because she was a woman, they discounted her views. Nevertheless, Hutchinson is a hero of American history, a trailblazer who existed during a time when women weren't supposed to blaze trails. Boston's authorities did not put her on trial just because she was a heretic; they also challenged her and shunned her because was a woman.

Toward the end of her trial, Hutchinson told her accusers, "You have power over my body but the Lord Jesus hath power over my body and soul." That statement is in many ways the crux of her relationship with God. She was certain that God lived and breathed inside of her, which rendered what "man" might do to her unimportant. And according to Stephen Prothero, professor of religion at Boston University, how Hutchinson spoke about her faith was a foreshadowing of what and how Americans would think and believe about God in the future. According to Prothero, "[Hutchinson was] the future in the sense of this, 'Religion really happens inside us,' you know, 'the drama is inside us. And God can speak to any of us.'"[8] Truthfully, John Winthrop was not battling with only Hutchinson; he was also fighting against her God, a deity he did not understand or know or want running around his neighborhood, inspiring others to think they were above the rules of his church.

Anne Hutchinson's God would soon become a bigger part of America's God, a God defined by personal interaction, a God who wanted to live within the very souls of people, a God who was more flexible and more easily shaped into what people needed God to be. On the horizon was a spiritual awakening that would help to make Hutchinson's God the God of the American people. Hutchinson's impact on American religion and culture is incalculable, but her experiences would begin a ripple effect in American history, one that would continue to grow and gain popularity. However, in 1637, Americans weren't ready for a personal God who lived inside their bodies; they wanted a God they could protect, one they could keep under house arrest, and one who worked on their society's behalf.

.   .   .

For the time being, the Puritans' God reigned supreme in America. That is because the Puritans were quite particular about whom they permitted to hold the reins. One well-known Puritan God-protector who kicked America's ass on more than a few occasions was Pastor Samuel Danforth, the minister who, for a time, led Roxbury Church in Boston. In 1670, Danforth was invited to preach a sermon before the delegates of the Bay Colony's General Court.

"What is it that distinguisheth New England from other colonies and plantations in America?" Danforth shouted at the room full of important men. The answer was obvious, of course; the Puritans were "God's faithful prophets," not to mention, the "fruition of His holy ordinance." In other words, unlike all of the other white Europeans who crossed over the Atlantic, the

Puritans were God's people and as God's people they had a responsibility. But according to Danforth, the Puritan men who governed over the colony's official affairs had lost their way, and consequently, God's way. As far as he was concerned, they were acting like Baptists.

"It is high time for us to remember whence we are fallen," Danforth told Boston's leaders, "and repent, and do our first works." The "first works" Danforth alludes to is this: Build the Kingdom of God. Right before his conclusion he quoted from the Gospel of Matthew, chapter six: "Seek ye first the Kingdom of God, and his Righteousness, and all these things shall be added unto you." Anytime Puritans heard the phrase "Kingdom of God," the general assumption was that God's Kingdom was meant to be a Puritan kingdom. Not an Anglican kingdom. Not a Quaker kingdom. Not even a Christian kingdom. They sought to establish a Puritan realm. And knowing that, Danforth offered his best advice for making this kingdom a reality. "If the people cleave to the Lord," he said, "[and] to his Prophets, and to his Ordinances, it will strike such a fear into the hearts of enemies, that they will be at their wits ends, and not know what to do." So basically he said: *Come on, Puritans, we are Puritans and God loves Puritans. So let's be the most Puritan Puritans ever—so* Puritan *that we send all non-Puritans (our enemies!) running away scared and signing up for extended stays at insane asylums.* Making enemies run scared was highly important to the Puritans, mostly because they believed that they could discern whether or not they were in God's goodwill by the successes or failures of their enemies.[9]

Loving their enemies wasn't even on the Puritans' radar. That's because loving their enemies didn't ensure that God would remain uniquely Puritan. Loving the Quakers was too risky. Loving the Anglicans was out of the question. Loving those with whom they vehemently disagreed might cause them to lose all that they had, their land, their control, their territories, their God.

To that end, the Puritans stooped to new lows when dealing with Mary Dyer, a Puritan woman who, after the Hutchinson trial, followed Anne to Rhode Island. After Hutchinson's passing, Dyer converted to Quakerism while on holiday in England. Knowing that Boston had recently passed a new law banning all Quakers, the feisty preacher returned to Massachusetts in 1658 to rain down her message of God on their anti-Quaker law. Her actions caused her to be banned a second time. But she was determined, and in 1660, Dyer returned once more to the colony she had once called home. However, that would be her final trip, not because the Puritans accepted her into their communal fold but because soon after her arrest she was sentenced to death and hanged on Boston Common.

The Puritan God was safe once more.

. . .

At the beginning of the eighteenth century, even though God had been living in the New World for more than seventy years, he still smelled like a European. Though Baptists, Quakers, Anglicans, and Presbyterians (among others) flocked to America's shores and colonized places like Virginia, Pennsylvania, and New Jersey, these religious sects failed to possess the structure, unity, and theology that could, like the Puritans, command the presence of God. For the most part, America's God was still wearing the same Augustinian-Calvinist garb he had donned when he arrived in Boston many years before.

The Puritan mind-set cannot be underestimated. God's involvement in their lives was not simply a means for engaging spirituality. It was etched into every facet of their existence, a practical (and impractical) set of guidelines that they prided themselves in keeping. Former Harvard University professor Perry Miller called the Puritans' wherewithal a "single intelligence," and believed that that unity created an "equilibrium of forces, emotional and intellectual, within the Puritan creed."[10] It was their dedication to that single frame of thinking—that Puritan creed, as Miller describes it—that caused them to become a force whose influence, despite their eventual demise, bled into the roots of American culture. That creed also became the foundation on which God in America would begin his westernized reign.

That said, God was also beginning to suffer under the Puritanical lifestyle. One glaring symptom was a severe cultural battle with anxiety. Onetime professor of history at Yale University Edmund Morgan believed that "lifelong anxiety and self-deprecation became hallmarks" of the Puritan life in America. This, Morgan suggests, is in direct contrast to the Puritan narratives of those who remained in England. "[In England], where Puritans had to contend against a hostile government and established church or else (during their years of triumph) against a host of heresies, believers found a haven of certainty in their personal dealings with God." Morgan purports that the true paradox is found in how individuals wrote about the hardships of their experiences, their narratives including a "passing through tribulations of spirit to find rest and contentment in some inner assurance of salvation. American Puritans had plenty of tribulations to record, but in their narratives the tribulations never end, the doubts never cease."[11]

But it was the Puritans' form of grace that ultimately crippled their way forward.

The makeup of God's grace is a topic that Americans have argued about since our beginning. While Christians of all varieties embrace God's grace as a core element of their Christian identity, Calvinists have, throughout America's story, held on to grace like they own the copyright. From the moment they landed in the New World, the Puritans certainly acted like they were the chief executives of the grace of God. In fact, many modern Calvinists attempt to command grace's definitions, wield who is and who isn't included, and wage spiritual warfare with whoever's grace does not seem as manly or narrow or Calvinistic as their own.

Today's Reformed thinkers no doubt celebrate the grace of God. Some of them actually seem to worship the grace that Calvinism invented. And sometimes grace just seems to make them into angry people who grip God in the clutches of their fists.

Many Calvinists today celebrate grace like hunters celebrating a fresh kill, jumping proudly around it like it's a carcass that they own and fully intend to cut up, freeze, and eventually eat. Sometimes they stuff it or hang it in their offices so others can see and enjoy from afar the grace they shot and killed. Calvinists aren't exactly selfish with grace; they just know that hunted "grace" is an acquired taste and not intended for everybody.

That's why the likes of Rob Bell get labeled heretical by Calvinists. Because a big grace paralyzes a Reformer's religious views. It diminishes their core responsibility, really, the one they spend a lot of time doing—policing the grace of God, enforcing its limitations, and ensuring that anybody who might consider believing outside the boundaries they have put on God's grace will feel like they are outside of God's grace. They are in many respects like the king's guard, seemingly willing to go to great lengths to ensure that nobody imagines grace any bigger than they do. Because how they imagine it is how God imagines it; at least that's what they assume. Perhaps this is why it's difficult to be a Calvinist in America. Because, as the Puritans learned, it's impossible to keep God on lockdown among people who are free.

CHAPTER THREE

GOD IN THE HANDS OF ANGRY PEOPLE

America's Christians have much to say about hell. The most familiar Christian understanding of hell is that it's an enormous pit of fire, a place of anguish and suffering that God has reserved for those who haven't accepted Jesus as their Lord and Savior. Christians differ on hell's details. Some think that America's good and merciful God will punish unrepentant sinners for eternity, while others suggest the persecution will be quick yet final, and still others hope that if hell exists, it will offer nonbelievers the opportunity for rehabilitation, perhaps a twelve-step program for those who desire to make something of themselves once and for all. And some Christians don't believe in hell at all, suggesting that God will ultimately redeem all of us.

Author Bill Wiese visited hell in 1988. Not surprising, the onetime real estate broker says it's an awful place, an experience that nobody in their right mind would ever want to risk waking up in. Which is exactly what happened to Wiese, according to his *New York Times* bestselling "true story" *23 Minutes in Hell*. God woke him up out of a dead sleep and plopped him down into one of hell's prison cells.

While much of Wiese's account reads like satire, the author and speaker swears every word is true, even the parts where God introduces him to some of hell's monsters, hideous creatures that sound like something Gandalf battles in Tolkien's tales of Middle Earth. "I was not alone in this cell," Wiese wrote. "I saw two enormous beasts.... The first one had bumps and scales all over its grotesque body. It had a huge protruding jaw, gigantic teeth, and large sunken-in eyes.... The second beast was taller and thinner, with very long arms and razor-sharp fins that covered its body."[1] Wiese's account is unbelievable, really, even though the author claims that every detail is supported with a verse or two from the Bible. However, most Americans have never experienced hell, at least not anything like Wiese described. The closest most of us have come to hell is standing in line at the DMV, where we've no doubt come in contact with a few government employees who we'd swear were demonic. Yet even our worst DMV experiences pale in comparison to the supernatural hell that Wiese swears he experienced in 1988.

Yet despite the fact that none of us have experienced hell, the majority of us believe in it. In a 2004 poll, Gallup found that 70 percent of Americans believe in hell, up from 56 percent in 1997.[2]

Francis Chan, a well-known evangelical Bible teacher and onetime megachurch pastor, seems to think that we Christians need hell. "Hell is the backdrop that reveals the profound and unbelievable grace of the cross," Chan wrote in his book *Erasing Hell.* "[Hell] brings to light the enormity of our sin and therefore portrays the undeserved favor of God in full color." According to Chan, hell is the grace of God; without it, comprehending the cross of Christ would be impossible. Chan's doctrine is a mouthful, partly because it elevates hell to an equal or greater value than Jesus's crucifixion. Furthermore, his words seem to undermine the resurrection of Jesus, the pivotal tenet of most Christian faiths, the miraculous event that conquered sin, death, judgment, and hell. Nonetheless, Chan's understanding of hell is the doctrine that most American evangelical believers embrace, a tormenting ideology rooted deeply in our country's history. Americans didn't invent hell—the concept has existed for generations in a myriad of forms—we just popularized it. Because Chan might be right. America's God needs hell. Without it, God might not exist.

. . .

On the eve of the eighteenth century, America and God were in trouble. That's hardly shocking, since God and America are always in trouble. One of the common themes throughout American Christian history is that God and America are usually sleeping in separate bedrooms. And it's always America's fault.

That's the message that America's clergy seem to echo over and over again, that America and God are on the outs. If you listen to preachers and Christian leaders, the relationship is never on par with how it was fifty years earlier. That's been true since America and God first hooked up. According to somebody somewhere, America is always on the verge of letting God become extinct or God is always on the verge of putting America out of its godless misery.

The Puritans were masters at creating tension between God and the American people. Beginning in the 1660s, Puritan clergy began doing just that: publicly denouncing the way Americans were treating God. Or as historian Thomas S. Kidd tells it, America's religious leaders were "lamenting the decline of their godly experiment."[3]

Of course, the Puritans were unusually gifted at bemoaning the status quo. Like Pat Robertson or Glenn Beck, America's seventeenth-century holy men were hell-bent on finding the darkest thread to every one of America's divine stories. However, unlike Robertson and Beck, the Puritans' habit for griping and complaining served a sincere purpose. "[Because] to expect revival," writes Kidd, "one had to experience despair."

By the late seventeenth century, the Puritan leadership had reason to be concerned about their people's future. Puritanism was no longer the pure religious piety it had once boasted. The World—the *New* World—with all of its worldliness, had crept in on God's plan, allowing hints of pluralism to seep into their doctrine and leading a multitude of Puritan people to run away from God.

According to Puritan ministers, despair often involved the actions of other Puritans. One such reverend was Michael Wigglesworth, who became so gravely concerned about the state of God and God's people that he wrote a poem called "God's Controversy with New England." Through Wigglesworth, God declared unto all backslidden Puritans that

> *Your sins me press as sheaves do load a cart,*
> *And therefore I will plague you for this gear*
> *Except you seriously, and soon, repent,*
> *I'll not delay your pain and heavy punishment.*[4]

Shockingly, God's great controversy in New England had nothing to do with Wigglesworth's sorry excuse for poetry, but rather with what he believed God was planning to do to the growing number of Puritan apostates. Wigglesworth was not the only one announcing God's forthcoming damnation. A multitude of preachers, Puritan and otherwise, joined the cause, shouting, writing, and rhyming bold admonitions. While their woes and warnings caused mild spiritual stirrings, the culture's morality continued to wane, deepening their throes of despair. The truth was becoming abundantly clear: America's God was in trouble.

"Christianity was not particularly popular in the New World

colonies." That's how Stephen Prothero explains it. In *American Jesus*, the author writes that "spiritual indifference was the rule in seventeenth-century Virginia, Maryland, New York, New Jersey, Delaware, and North and South Carolina. In all these places, churchgoers were rare and churches scarce."[5]

Was Puritanism dying? That's what many believed. Though Puritanism's ideals, methods, and values would continue to influence the American story for centuries to come, as our young country inched toward the new century, society was not brimming with religion and spirituality the way preachers like Samuel Danforth and Cotton Mather believed it should be.

What was the disconnect between America and God? For one thing, Calvinism's God wasn't connecting with America's common folk. Even those who wanted to experience God struggled to engage the God that the majority of American preachers were advertising in their churches. The problem was that John Calvin's God, while he thrived in the heady halls of universities and among New England's aristocrats, did not fare as well among simpletons, farmers, moderately educated folks, and small-town residents. Regular people couldn't relate to Calvinism's God. He was too dark, too esoteric, too stuffy, and still much too British. Also, many Americans wondered, "what was the point?"

As you may know or have experienced, America's God always provides the answer to our tough questions, or at the very least he provides a man who's convinced he knows the answer to our tough questions. In 1703, God provided the latter. He created Jonathan Edwards, a minister far too intelligent for his own good. But under the influence of Edwards, God would begin to morph into the American deity that many of us know today.

. . .

A short time after Jonathan Edwards was born, rumors began spreading that in some parts of America, colonials were experiencing spiritual renewal. In 1705, Samuel Danforth seemed nearly giddy about what was happening at his church in Taunton, Massachusetts, writing that "we are much encouraged by an unusual and amazing Impression, made by GOD'S SPIRIT on all Sorts among us, especially on the young Men and Women."[6] Though grateful for the success, Danforth hoped and believed that what he was experiencing was only the beginning, a Holy Spirit prequel for what was to come. "The Time of the pouring out of the SPIRIT upon all Flesh, may be at the Door. Let's be earnest in Prayer that CHRIST's Kingdom may come."[7]

Meanwhile, Jonathan Edwards was turning nine years old, and all signs pointed to the fact that the only son of Timothy and Esther Edwards (they had eleven children) was unnaturally brilliant. In addition to smarts, Edwards also possessed an enthralling passion for God. "My sense of divine things gradually increased," he wrote in his diary, "and became more and more lively, and had more of that inward sweetness."[8] That's how Edwards described the astute spirituality of his youth, like a man destined to become the eighteenth century's Captain Kangaroo. Nonetheless, that "inward sweetness" awakened the future preacher to a rather uncommon youthful aptitude for holiness.

Shortly after his ninth birthday, Edwards experienced an uncanny meeting with God, an encounter he called a "season of awakening." That moment left a lasting impression on the prodigy. For more than nine months, young Edwards prayed in secret five times a day. He engaged his friends in conversations about God, even assembling groups for meetings of prayer and Bible study. "My mind was much engaged in it," he wrote. And like all devout Calvinists, his actions brought him "much self-righteous pleasure."[9] But as George Marsden points out, "An 'awakening' was no guarantee of salvation."[10] Edwards was a

Calvinist after all, the kind rooted in Puritanism; God made few guarantees. And much to Edwards's and God's chagrin, the poor kid soon "lost all of those affections and delights" and, as he put it, "returned like a dog to its vomit."[11]

Eventually, God's last Puritan, as many consider him, turned away from his own retch and back to the things of God. When he was thirteen, Edwards enrolled at Yale, where in addition to theology he became engulfed in the study of natural history, atomic theory, and science. While he excelled in all of his studies, he was truly gifted at one: writing. As a graduate student he dreamed of one day wowing the world with his gift. In one of his notebooks, he listed his rules for writing. Rule number six:

The world will expect more modesty because of my circumstances—in America, young, etc. Let there be a superabundance of modesty, and though perhaps 'twill otherwise be needless, it will wonderfully make way for its reception in the world. Mankind are by nature proud and exceeding envious, and ever jealous of such upstarts; and it exceedingly irritates and affronts 'em to see 'em appear in print. Yet the modesty ought not to be affected and foolish, but decent and natural.[12]

That was Edwards's way of practicing his humility in front of a mirror. Even with only a handful of preaching gigs under his belt, God's American Sweetheart already sounds like the perfect evangelical pastor. Had he been born today, Edwards would likely be famous on the Internet, uploading his spiritual intellect onto YouTube and telecasting it around the world.

Five years later, in 1728, Jonathan Edwards became the pastor of a church in Northampton, Massachusetts. This was where the feisty young preacher would begin to truly test his skill as a spiritual orator. His depth of wisdom about God and the world was wildly different from the onset. That, in addition to his gift for communicating God to the people, was a ministerial package that few congregants had experienced before. Edwards immediately began putting his "gifts" to work. Four years later, the young pastor noted in his personal journal that change was in the air.

. . .

Jonathan Edwards is one of the most misunderstood individuals in American history. Which might be one of the reasons we still talk about him. Some people praise him for his near-divine understanding of God and theology, while others loathe him for personifying everything they hate about American Christianity. He was a complex individual. But those who play leading roles in the drama of American Christianity usually are complicated creatures.

Whatever you think to be true about Edwards, whether you consider him a saint or a spiritual psychopath or a variety of both, it's impossible to deny his extraordinary influence on America's understanding of God, hell, and faith. Prior to Edwards's gambling his career for the topic of hell, his words and wisdom helped people see God. And what a God it was, too. Edwards's God was glorious, full of beauty, and seemingly uninterested in making people feel insecure. God was bigger, more glorious under Edwards's watch.

What made Edwards's theology more than just theology was his poetic language. People did not simply read or hear the words of Jonathan Edwards, they felt them. And in some cases, people felt the words before they even understood them. Edwards was a mystic, a man who didn't simply write or preach about God, he experienced him. "And as I was walking there," he wrote after having a spiritual vision, "and looked up on the sky and clouds; there came into my mind, a sweet sense of the glorious majesty and grace of God, that I know not how to express."[13] Here Edwards was trying hard to be humble. Because in truth, he knew exactly how to express what he saw. In fact, he was building an entire career on expressing with words his vast mastery of the wonder and majesty of God.

Sure, nobody knew if he was actually correct about God or not. That's where the faith part came in. But considering that his audience was made up of men and women who'd survived Puritanism, in all likelihood they wanted to believe him. They hoped that he was right. Because most of the people who heard or read Edwards's words about God had never heard of such a God, an American God that was "in a sweet conjunction: majesty and meekness joined together: it was a sweet and gentle, and holy majesty; and also a majestic meekness; an awful sweetness; a high, and great, and holy gentleness."[14] Compared to the God that most of them had been subjected to, Edwards's God sounded, well, almost divine. George Marsden writes that "it was only when Jonathan's vision expanded to appreciate that the triune God who controlled this vast universe must be ineffably good, beautiful, and loving beyond human comprehension that he could lose himself in God."[15]

Even though Edwards is often considered America's last Puritan, he wasn't a full-on Puritan, at least not like John Winthrop or John Cotton. While he was no doubt affected by his heritage, his understanding of God was not stereotypical. The most telling difference was that he viewed God as both grandiose and personal, once writing that "there came into my soul...a sense of the glory of the Divine Being; a new sense quite different from anything I ever experienced before."[16]

Edwards's perspectives about God seem softer than those held by his dead forefathers. His approach seems more akin to Anne Hutchinson's, a theology cushioned with a bigger helping of divine love and blessing than the Puritans, who seemed to think of God as a colossal warden of the jail known as Earth. How Edwards described God's acclaim was unlike most before him, melding conservative theology with mystical revelations, spiritual pluses he called "the river of God's pleasures." It's likely that what he stated was compounded in the minds of his congregants by *how he stated it*, a poetic language that made God seem almost huggable. In fact, his finesse for language was what set him apart from his contemporaries, and he is considered by many to be one of America's greatest writers. Edwards's skill with words helped him launch the eighteenth century's "New Calvinism," a born-again message that not only paid respect to the rich doctrine of John Calvin, but regenerated a lust within people to know God, *feel* God, and become moved to pursue living everyday holiness.

> What it is to be pure in heart...that to be pure in heart, is the sure way to gain [God's] blessedness...that is the only way....Purity of heart is here to be understood in distinction from a mere external purity, or a purity of the outward actions and behavior...he is pure in heart, who chooses and takes the greatest delight in spiritual enjoyment... [and] hungers and thirsts after the pure light of the new Jerusalem.[17]

According to Edwards, God's interests were changing, moving away from being preoccupied with humanity's physicality to that of humanity's heart, desiring to fill their emotional and spiritual beings with joy and contentment. Today, thinking about the heart is a common practice among Christians. But in Edwards's day, heart lingo was a novel concept. This was how he helped to shape American Christianity, affecting how Americans would not only talk about God but feel connected to God. Because of Edwards, a knowledge-based *Puritan* God became a heart-focused *American* God, and rather than inviting people to *know about* God, Edwards became one of the first to invite people to *experience* God.

. . .

As Edwards felt "change in the air" stirring among the people at his Northampton church, those glimpses foreshadowed what would later—actually not until the nineteenth century, in fact—be called the Great Awakening (Part One), a spiritual revival that began in the 1730s and peaked at some point in the early to mid-1740s. Some historians believe that history has exaggerated the effects of this American revival, which is likely true; however, even though the "Awakening" probably wasn't as widespread as once assumed, Edwards's preaching indeed launched a spiritual renewal in his town, a God-sanctioned resurgence that indeed began to spread.

During his early tenure at Northampton, Edwards became concerned about his town's youth and their carelessness about spiritual matters. "Licentious and immoral practices seem to get great head amongst young people," he preached. "And how little appearance is there of a spirit of seriousness and religion to be seen among them? How little concern about their salvation and escaping eternal misery?"[18] To that end, he began looking for opportunities to reach young people.

In the spring of 1734, the untimely death of a young man became a catalyst for Edwards to reach Northampton's youth. At the young man's funeral, Edwards preached a sermon that, for him, turned into a memorial service for every soul in attendance:

> Consider, if you should die in youth...when others stand
> by your bedside and see you gasping and breathing your

last or...see you put into the coffin and behold the awful visage which death has given you, how shocking will it be to them to think this is the person that used to be so vain and frothy in conversation. This is he that was so lewd a companion. This is he that used to spend of his time in his leisure hours so much in frolicking.[19]

Believe it or not, those dark words knocked 'em dead, which was exactly his intention. Writing a short time later, Edwards noted that many of his youngest members "clearly exemplified" what he called the universal holiness of life, which he believed was "intuitive and immediate evidence" that somebody had awakened to God.[20]

The more spiritual successes that Edwards experienced, the more he seemed to intentionally infuse his sermons with language deemed to move a person's emotional center—their souls—to spiritually respond. And they did respond. In fact, some of them were so stirred by Edwards's words that they started showing physical signs of God's Spirit dwelling among them.

In the early summer of 1741, Edwards wrote, "[I preached a sermon] to a company at a private house. Near the conclusion of the exercise one or two persons that were professors were so greatly affected with a sense of the greatness and glory of divine things, and the infinite importance of the things of eternity, that they were not able to conceal it; the affection of their minds overcoming their strength, and having a very visible effect on their bodies."

Edwards called these physical symptoms to his preaching "the Affections," bodily manifestations that he describes in such a way that they sound more like symptoms caused by zombie bites than the Spirit of God. "Many of the young people and children appeared to be overcome with a sense of the greatness and glory of divine things...and many others at the same time were overcome with distress about their sinful and miserable state and condition; so that the whole room was full of nothing but outcries, faintings and such like."[21]

Once, the Affections spread while Edwards was teaching the children of his church. According to Edwards, "The children there were very generally and greatly affected with the warnings and counsels that were given them...the room was filled with cries: and when they were dismissed, they, almost all of them, went home crying aloud through the streets, to all parts of the town."[22]

Who was creating these Affections? The Holy Spirit? Jonathan Edwards? The Early American Crypt? At times, Edwards seemed to almost be testing his spiritual gift for language, examining what would happen if he did *A* and how it would affect *B*, and then recording the results. After engaging the youngest children, Edwards tested his words on the sixteen- to twenty-six-year-olds. That gathering, like the others, also went better than he expected. By the time he finished talking, the Affections were everywhere. "Many seemed to be very greatly and most agreeably affected," Edwards wrote. "[They were feeling] humility, self-condemnation, self-abhorrence."[23]

By his accounts, the summer of 1741 was a happy time for Edwards. The Spirit of God really seemed to be working overtime in Northampton and the surrounding communities. Edwards recorded numerous events in which results included some combination of fainting, convulsions, seizures, distress, love, trembling, groans, agonies of body, humility, the failing of bodily strength, and terrible, heartwrenching outcries of terror.

And yet, without question, Edwards saw that it was all good.

Jonathan Edwards wasn't the only one helping to spread the Affections. Jonathan Parsons, a New England reverend who became a traveling preacher during the First Awakening, also saw signs of human calamity, a soulful distress that seemed to make him almost giggle with glee. "Many had their countenances changed," he wrote in his journal, "their thoughts seemed to trouble them, so that the joints of their loins were loosed, and their knees smote one against another. Great numbers cried out aloud in the anguish of their souls. Several stout men fell as though a cannon had been discharged; and a ball had made its way through their hearts. Some young women were thrown into hysteric fits."[24]

America's God was becoming brazen, quickly breaking free from its uppity Old World ways and venturing out into unfamiliar spiritual territory.

. . .

By the summer of 1741, many people across New England were experiencing the Affections. Edwards couldn't deny that he was right smack in the middle of a formidable spiritual rekindling, which meant he needed to seize the moment while everybody was still drunk with God.

On July 8, Edwards traveled to the town of Enfield, Connecticut. He'd been invited to preach because some of Enfield's holier residents were concerned that the Affections had as of yet passed over their town like the angel of death. According to one of the concerned few, the most they'd managed to muster out of their local heathens was some "considerable crying among the people" and bit of "screeching in the streets."[25] That simply wasn't good enough. They wanted the people of their town to experience whatever was happening in places like Suffield, Longmeadow, and Coventry, locations where the Affections had hit people like an atom bomb and proceeded to induce seizures, night sweats, and fits of rage. So they contacted Edwards and assigned to him a clear mission: Bring the Affections to Enfield.

Chances are, upon receiving his marching orders, Edwards likely knew which sermon he was going to preach, an effective number he'd delivered once before called "Sinners in the Hands of an Angry God."

According to legend, the moment Edwards started preaching, a morbid hush fell over the crowd at Enfield. One admirer described Edwards's delivery as solemn. "His words were so full of ideas, set in such a plain and striking light, that few speakers have been so able to demand the attention of an audience as he."[26] On that day Edwards preached from a text in the Book of Deuteronomy (32:35): "To me belongeth vengeance and recompence; their foot shall slide in due time: for the day of their calamity is at hand, and the things that shall come upon them make haste."

With a calm and matter-of-fact demeanor, Edwards told the people of Enfield that God stood ready to toss their meaningless sin-ridden souls into a black hole of fiery torment, a terrible place where Satan waited and gleefully pined for the chance to manifest his dominion over their bodies. Edwards described God as like a mean-spirited child, one who plays sadist with a granddaddy longlegs, blissfully tearing its legs off its body and then holding it over a hot flame, teasing the creature with suffering and torment.

The picture that Edwards painted was horrendous and frightening, a duty he performed with ease, as if he'd gone on a field trip to hell a couple days before with his kids, witnessed its horror, and on the way home stopped at Olive Garden. But that's how Edwards viewed hell, as if it were a geographical location. To all who were cramped inside the Enfield church, Edwards's words brought hell to life, making it real, tangible, and terrifying, like France or New Jersey or a Carnival cruise to Cozumel.

In *Erasing Hell*, Francis Chan writes, "God is love, but [God] also defines what love is. We don't have the license to define love according to our standards." If Chan is correct, this is how Jonathan Edwards defined the love of God in 1741:

> The God that holds you over the pit of Hell, much as one holds a spider, or some loathsome insect, over the fire, abhors you, and is dreadfully provoked; his wrath towards you burns like fire; he looks upon you as worthy of nothing else, but to be cast into the fire; he is of purer eyes than to bear to have you in his sight; you are ten thousand times so abominable in his eyes as the most hateful venomous serpent is in ours. You have offended him infinitely more than ever a stubborn rebel did his prince: and yet 'tis nothing but his hand that holds you from falling into the fire every moment: 'tis to be ascribed to nothing else, that you did not go to Hell the last night...but that God's hand has held you up: there is no other reason to be given why you han't gone to Hell since you have sat here in the house of God, provoking his pure eyes by your sinful wicked manner of attending his solemn worship: yea, there is nothing else that is to be given as a reason why you don't this very moment drop down into Hell. Oh sinner! Consider the fearful danger you are in.

Even in context, taking on the presence of an individual from Enfield, Connecticut, in 1741—somebody who believes in God, the Bible, and hell and was present on July 8 to hear Edwards expound—this prose, though lavishly adorned with glorious illustrations, perfect sentence structure, and a creative mix of Edwards's writing brilliance and his ability to use simple language that the common man could relate to, was a vile, reprehensible excuse for a sermon. And yet the worst part of this gruesome diatribe is not the parts about hell, it's the sentiments that Edwards makes about God. Edwards made God into a monster, a horrible creature reminiscent of the beasts that scared Bill Wiese when he visited hell in 1988.

But for Edwards, his "Angry God" presentation was a success. The Affections fell over the crowd that night, most attendees either screaming, shaking, having convulsions, fainting, howling, moaning, or experiencing uncontrollable fits of terror. In fact, Edwards's words caused such a ruckus that he wasn't able to finish his sermon. The one slightly hopeful line at the end didn't even get spoken. Instead, the residents of Enfield were left dangling like spiders over the pits of hell that night, overcome with the spirit of Edwards's "Affections."

Jonathan Edwards offered a multitude of thoughts regarding hell, judgment, and the wrath of God. In addition to "Angry God," other sermons included "The Justice of God in the Damnation of Sinners," "The Torments of Hell Are Exceedingly Great," and "God Is Very Angry at the Sins of Children." In the latter, Edwards had invited all of the children in his church to come up front for a special children's message. Once the little ones were all gathered around his feet, he offered the following words:

> God is not only angry enough to correct you, but to cast you into Hell to all eternity. You deserve to burn in Hell forever. Your being children doesn't excuse you. Though [you] haven't so much knowledge, yet you know better.... Wicked children are in God's sight like young serpents. We hate young snakes. They are the children of the devil. God hates the devil, so he abhors his children. The devil is the old serpent and wicked children are his children.[27]

And the Affections spread.

・　・　・

One day God will officially survive Jonathan Edwards. Some might argue that he doesn't have to. But that, quite honestly, undermines the roles that humanity plays in telling and defining God's story. While it's unfair to pigeonhole Edwards simply as a mean, hell-obsessed preacher, it's also impossible to separate his more Affections-driven banter from the richer, more heartfelt theologies that he was also known for writing and preaching.

Throughout his career, Edwards's greatest battle was an inward struggle with self-glorification; he once wrote that he was "greatly afflicted with a proud and self-righteous spirit." Comparing pride to a serpent, he admitted—and was confronted by others—that his pride was constantly "rising and putting forth its head, continually, everywhere."[28] Throughout my study of Edwards, especially while reading his personal reflections, I often sensed that he became personally obsessed with spreading the Affections. On one hand he did not fully grasp why people responded as they did to his sermons, but then again, he liked it. And so rather than focus his message on the things of God, he began to focus on the results. And sadly, when it comes to preaching religion, you catch a whole lot more souls with hell than you do with the glory of God.

Jonathan Edwards changed the story of America's God. He changed how the people of his time engaged God, editing a theology that was often portrayed harshly and dogmatically. He made strides to shape it with words into an almost beloved relationship between a grandiose God and a broken and depraved American heart. His words set the stage for what would become a steady foundation for America's God to revolt against the Old World and bring about revolution. Historian Perry Miller suggests that America's Enlightenment began and ended with Jonathan Edwards. And Edwards played a most defining role in bridging the space between Puritanism and what would eventually become American evangelicalism.

It was Edwards's talent as a writer that, on one hand, makes him unforgettably important to so many still today. Preachers like John Piper, Tim Keller, Mark Driscoll, and others wouldn't have much to write or preach about without Edwards dedicating the majority of his existence to literally emoting his version of John Calvin's God onto the page. But it's that same talent, that profound ability to create rich imagery with sentences and paragraphs, that would ultimately backfire on him. Rather than his gift becoming defined by his thoughts on God's glory or God's beauty, Edwards's words helped to Americanize God's hell, turning this country's doctrines about hell into HELL™. Hell was dark and gloomy enough; HELL™ would eventually become a method for introducing millions to God.

In 1742, shortly before Edwards was set to leave on an eight-stop preaching tour of Massachusetts and Connecticut, he fellowshipped with his friend the Reverend Joseph Bellamy. Though younger than Edwards and well known for his boisterous, witty demeanor, Bellamy was one of Edwards's closest companions. During their meeting, Edwards divulged all that God was doing. After mourning the slight religious decline in Northampton but reveling in the success of his church's work with the town's children, he showcased much enthusiasm about how God was faring in America and around the world. "The work of God is greater at this day in the land, than it has been at any time," he told his friend.

And furthermore, he said, "Neither Earth or Hell can hinder [God's] work that is going on in the country."[29]

CHAPTER FOUR

THE EVANGELICALS ARE COMING!

"Jesus is my husband." This is how my friend Caroline described her relationship with Jesus Christ in 2003, as if the two had decided to settle down and purchase his and hers bath towels. Caroline is one of those people whose faith seems almost otherworldly, annoyingly so. She wears Christian shirts, carries pocketbooks with scripture verses printed on their sides, hums hymns, and possesses a positive outlook on everything. Though I've grown accustomed to her spiritualized nature, the one thing about Caroline that makes me want to drink is how often she name-drops Jesus in conversations. For instance, if she asks me how I'm doing and I say, "Fine," her response is, "Praise Jesus." Or once, as I was telling her about my friend Jim, who at the time was battling an infection he'd picked up on a missionary trip to Indonesia, rather than simply listening, Caroline punctuated every one of my sentences with whispers of Jesus's name. When I told her that Jim was helping to fund the digging of a well in Indonesia, she put a "Bless him, Jesus" on the end of my sentence. Or as I was sharing about the symptoms Jim was experiencing, she added, "Oh, help him Jesus," or "Heal him in Jesus's name" in between each one.

I'm not offended by her incessant mentioning of Jesus, but

sometimes her Christ-centered interjections don't match up with the emotional tone of a conversation. Sometimes she will praise Jesus when she should be crying Jesus, or she will sigh Jesus when smiling or shouting Jesus with emphasis would be more appropriate. I've never mentioned it to her for fear that it might be a neurological disorder, like a form of Tourette's that causes her to involuntarily and sometimes inappropriately use the name of Jesus. Besides, if there's anybody who would find value in having Jesus as her tic, it would be Caroline.

I once ran into Caroline and a group of her church friends at a Christian gathering in Atlanta. During that fifteen-minute interaction, I realized that Caroline's tendency to whisper the name of Jesus in vain wasn't a neurological problem, at least not one that could be helped with medication. As the five of us chitchatted about the weather, the conference, and a sad story that one of them had read on a blog earlier that day, all around the circle Caroline and her friends whispered random, syrupy-sweet mentions of Jesus's name. They sighed Jesus. They praised Jesus. They invoked his name as a noun, as an adjective, and twice as a verb. A few minutes into that conversation the name above all names had been reduced to a tic, an annoying habit, a sound that was devoid of meaning and emotion.

Evangelicals using the name of Jesus in vain isn't new. For more than two hundred years, some of America's most impassioned believers have misused the name of Christ to advance kingdoms, manipulate masses, or showcase unequivocal devotion. However, in the early days of American evangelicalism, Americans rarely misused the name of Jesus. That's because Jesus wasn't hugely popular among America's faithful in the 1700s. They believed in Jesus, of course, in his death, burial, and resurrection. And they certainly uttered his name in liturgies and prayers. But among God's people, while they certainly believed that Jesus sat at the right hand of the Father, it was a very distant right. Stephen Prothero writes that "even church members were relatively uninterested in Jesus." And among Puritans, "Jesus was at best a marginal figure."[1] But that would soon change. In other words, by the middle of the eighteenth century, Jesus was on the verge of becoming an American icon, an idea that would demand our worship, a spiritual center that would become the focus of American Christianity, and a God-man whose name would become worthy of taking in vain.

· · ·

By the middle of the First Great Awakening, God had more American personalities than Jesus has nicknames at Christmastime. In New England, God was a Congregationalist, which meant he was a more open-minded and soon-to-be liberal Puritan. Even though the average Congregational attendee was stuffy, pious, white, and Puritan, God no doubt felt at home among people who celebrated him in an environment that was vacuum-sealed to keep out the Holy Spirit. Those who micromanaged the Congregational culture of God held him hostage within an intellectual setting. The only people who handled God were those who taught Bible courses at universities, possessed the "spiritual gift" for governing land and enforcing dogma, and felt fashionable wearing powdered wigs.

But God was also alive and well in the Delaware Valley, a deity known to the Quakers of Pennsylvania and New Jersey as the almighty omnipotent Friend. That's what the Religious Society of Friends (the formal name of the Quakers) called each other, Friends, because even back then the Quakers were, well, a little different.

Much to the frustration of every single colonial Protestant, Roman Catholics settled down with their God in Maryland. However, even though the Mid-Atlantic colony became a haven for Catholics, the God of Catholicism would have a very difficult journey adjusting to the widespread hatred and prejudice of anything remotely Catholic. Though Catholics eventually adjusted and found a home among the American dream, the deep-seated religious angst left over from the days of the Reformation would follow close behind for many generations. Eventually, Maryland became dominated by the Anglicans, the descendants of England's high church. Having already established their God as the God of Virginia and the Carolinas (and later, Georgia), they moved their deity into Maryland and immediately began enforcing laws.

Among the thirteen original colonies, God came in a wide and varied assortment. In New York, God was Dutch Reformed. In New Jersey, God was, in addition to being Quaker, Lutheran, Presbyterian, and Baptist. In Pennsylvania, God performed a multitude of wardrobe changes, from Amish to Brethren, from Lutheran to Baptist, from Mennonite to Reformed.

Unity among these varied God-ideals was almost nonexistent. Many of the settlers had either lost the vision of why their ancestors had moved out of the Old World or that vision had become edited by time, experience, and history. Amid the colonies (and the religious groups that settled in the colonies) there existed no common story, no unifying narrative that bound them together toward one purpose. At a macro level, America's colonies appeared dysfunctional, a chaos of ideas, beliefs, and purpose. That lack of vision, combined with no clear objective for what the American story was going to become, put their future as well as God's future at risk.

· · ·

In 1739, God showed up on a boat from England at the port in Philadelphia, except nobody noticed because the country was buzzing with excitement because evangelist George Whitefield was on the same boat. This was exciting news, mostly because Whitefield's reputation had arrived in America many weeks earlier. Even the likes of Benjamin Franklin and Jonathan Edwards were eager to see if the twenty-four-year-old Reformed Anglican lived up to the hype. Franklin had been following the news about Whitefield in the newspapers, seemingly impressed by the British revivalist's ability to create his own publicity. The word from the Old World was that thousands of people were filling up fields across Great Britain to hear Whitefield preach about what he called the "new birth." The rumor was that God had made Whitefield into a new being, given him a "new heart," and promised "to renew a right spirit within him." And according to Whitefield, God wanted to make the American people "new" too.

However, George Whitefield's American revivals were not the beginning of America's evangelicalism. Rumblings of evangelicalism were happening among the colonies as early as the 1680s. But Whitefield's arrival and mass appeal helped unify America's lesser evangelical movements into a larger idea, one that packed a bigger Gospel punch than it would have without him.[2]

In many ways George Whitefield's life defines American evangelicalism. A spiritual mystic who'd believed since he was a child that God had dreamed up something special for him, Whitefield constantly received positive messages and visions about himself from God. At the time, especially among clergy, dreams, visions, and "impressions" from God were a popular trend. Eventually, God gave Whitefield "an unaccountable, but very strong impression" that he should become a preacher.[3] So that's what Whitefield did; however, as much as he was a revivalist and preacher, he was also one hell of a salesman, a true showman who'd grown up in Great Britain's theater scene and understood the art of performance. That's not to say his Gospel was all theatrics. There were some theatrics, no doubt—he was a Calvinist after all—but Whitefield also believed every word he preached, certain beyond a shadow of a doubt that he was correct about God. "God had shown me what true religion was," Whitefield wrote. "It was a ray of Divine Light that instantaneously darted in upon my soul."[4] So upon its inhabiting Whitefield's stout frame, he and the Divine Light jumped on a boat and darted across the Atlantic with plans of going into all of the New World and preaching the "new birth" to every creature.

"New birth" wasn't a common idea among American believers in the early years of the eighteenth century. In fact, the message was new even for Whitefield. It wasn't until he attended Pembroke College, Oxford, that he learned that God had a rebirthing plan. There, the future evangelist became chummy with a group of pious "methodists," led by the Wesley brothers, John and Charles. The Wesley siblings gathered regularly with friends under the moniker "the Holy Club," and while in their company, Whitefield experienced the "new birth."[5] Later, when Whitefield's outdoor revivals took off in Great Britain, he asked Charles Wesley—the man who would one day become best known for authoring hymns such as "Christ the Lord Is Risen Today" and "O for a Thousand Tongues to Sing"—to take over his traveling mission while he and the Light gallivanted across America. But Wesley was uncertain at first.

"I could scarce reconcile myself at first to this strange way of preaching in the fields," Wesley wrote in his journal, believing that Whitefield's approach to reaching the masses was unconventional and therefore potentially heretical. "All my life...I should have thought the saving of souls almost a sin, if it had not been done in a church."[6] Even after Wesley agreed to preach Whitefield's British revivals, he still seemed unsure about it, writing that by filling in for Whitefield he'd "submitted to be more vile." It wasn't until he'd "proclaim in the highways the glad tidings of salvation" in front of "about three thousand people" that Wesley's preaching ego allowed him the grace to fully enjoy the experience.

Meanwhile, Whitefield and God were knocking 'em dead in America.

Benjamin Franklin was thoroughly impressed, despite steep disagreements with Whitefield concerning God. "The multitudes of sects and denominations that attended his sermons were enormous," wrote Franklin. "It was a matter of speculation to me...to observe the extraordinary influence of his oratory on his hearers, and how much they admired and respected him." The honor the crowds showed Whitefield seemed to surprise Franklin, especially considering "[Whitefield's] common abuse of them, assuring them they were naturally half Beasts and half Devils." But Franklin was willing to look past Whitefield's flaws, even his devout belief in Satan and the doctrine of depravity, both of which seemed cruel in Franklin's mind. "It was wonderful to see the change soon made in the manners of our inhabitants; from being thoughtless or indifferent about religion, it seemed as if all the world were growing religious...[and] one could not walk thro' the town without hearing Psalms sung in different families of every street." Whitefield's adventures had only begun and already his "Good News" was making the streets of Philly a sweeter experience for Franklin.

Franklin wasn't the only one to notice Whitefield's evangelical effect. In 1740, Whitefield finally met Jonathan Edwards. After hearing him preach, Esther Edwards, Jonathan's mother, said that Whitefield "cast a spell" over the people, and that excited her. Edwards commended Whitefield too, writing that "the minds of the people in general appeared more engaged in religion."[7]

From Pennsylvania and New Jersey to the Carolinas and Georgia, the man called a "pioneer in the commercialization of religion" and "Anglo-America's first religious celebrity"[8] captured hearts and ignited the spiritual imaginations of the American people. In truth, what sold Whitefield's God during the Awakening wasn't so much God as it was Whitefield. Compared to the preaching Americans were accustomed to hearing, Whitefield's style was most unique; he had an easy delivery, a tone and demeanor that delighted people's senses. That, combined with personal stories, a couple of one-liners, and the ability to sum up God's message in the form of one question—"What must I do to be saved?"—offered him the tools necessary to build a foundation upon which God could more easily evolve out of his Puritan heritage into an American evangelical divinity. Whitefield also opened God's doors to more people:

> And now let me address all of you high and low, rich and poor, one with another, to accept of mercy and grace while it is offered to you; Now is the accepted time, now is the day of salvation; and will you not accept it, now it is offered unto you?[9]

Soon, many Americans were able to answer that question with a resounding "Yes!" For the first time since colonization began, Americans from different backgrounds were agreeing to the same religious idea. Presbyterians stood alongside Baptists, who stood alongside Anglicans, who likely scooted over a few steps but still said "Yes!" to the spiritual message that Whitefield was selling.

· · ·

Not everybody was fond of George Whitefield's evangelical message. Some people thought his message of "new birth" was heresy. This was an anxiety for Whitefield. As far as he was concerned, the gap between those who believed in rebirth and those who did not was a canyon. "There is a fundamental difference between us and them. They believe only an outward Christ, we further believe that He must be inwardly formed in our hearts also."[10] Though Whitefield's Awakening unified people in some places, it also created deep and resentful separation between families, churches, and communities.[11] And sometimes the rifts turned ugly. Often during Whitefield's sermons, hecklers screamed, tossed tomatoes and peaches, and occasionally hurled the carcasses of dead animals at the evangelist.

Criticism bothered Whitefield, but he was also determined not to lose concentration, confiding in a friend, "If the Lord gives us a true catholic spirit, free from a party sectarian zeal, we shall do well...for I am persuaded, unless we all are content to preach Christ, and to keep off from disputable things, wherein we differ, God will not bless us long."[12]

. . .

At the peak of the Awakening, as Whitefield started moving his message into the seminaries and Congregational districts of New England, his ideas started changing. Suddenly God's big point went from "I will make you new" to exclaiming at Harvard and Yale that the scholar's "light had become darkness."[13] Whitefield's *new* message went over like infant Baptism among Baptists.

The controversy sparked by Whitefield's seminary appearances was heightened by the unruly actions of other evangelical preachers and itinerants who were waging what they considered heaven-sanctioned spiritual warfare against New England's religious elite. One of the soldiers was Gilbert Tennent. Months after Whitefield's visit, Tennent preached at Yale, telling students that their school was a den of "modern Pharisees" and "not to hide their dead hearts behind a veneer of scholarship." Then there was James Davenport, a squirrelly Presbyterian minister from Kentucky. A month or so after Tennent's tirade at Yale, Davenport stood in the pulpit of a New Haven church and referred to its preacher—the Reverend Joseph Noyes, who was sitting in the audience—as a "vicious 'wolf in sheep's clothing' and urged parishioners to separate from his ministry."[14] Davenport's appearance caused chaos to break out among Yale's students. Disrespect and behavior on the campus became so coarse and unruly that the president closed the school and sent them all home.

Toward the end of the Awakening, many of these contrary evangelicals came together under the moniker "the New Lights," a semi-organized group whose mission was to "denounce the Congregational ministry as apostate."[15] The worst of the "New Lights" was Davenport. In March 1743, the *Boston Weekly Post* reported (with much sarcasm) about the preacher's most "shining" and memorable performance, spearheading one of America's first public book burnings:

[At the] Conclusion of the Publick Worship, and also as the People were returning from the House of God, they were surpriz'd with a great noise and out-cry; Multitudes hasten'd toward...one of the most public Places in the Town, and there found these good People encompassing a Fire which they had built up in the Street, into which they were casting Numbers of Books, principally on Divinity, and those that were well-approved by Protestant Divines.[16]

But one book burning wasn't enough for Davenport; no, the relentless and fiery preacher led a second book burning the following day. In the middle of God's second bonfire of "Light,"

Davenport decided "that they themselves were guilty of idol-izing their Apparel" and they should take off "those things especially which were for ornament, and let them be burnt." But some of Davenport's followers weren't wearing anything they deemed "idol"-worthy, so they reverted to stripping off their clothes and casting the items into the fire. Then, after saying a prayer, Davenport tore off his "breeches [pants], and hove them with violence into the pile, saying, 'Go you with the rest.'" According to the *Boston Weekly Post*, the event concluded when a stranger came along and told Davenport that "the Devil was in him." Davenport agreed, telling the man that indeed he "was under the Influence of an evil Spirit, and that God had left Him." Davenport's unprecedented display of "faith-based evangelical crazy" caused many of his peers to question the preacher's mental state.

Watching today's evangelical lunacy unfold in front of us on blogs, Facebook, and CNN, it is certainly easy to relate. The only difference between today's crazy and what happened in 1743 is that Pastor Davenport was humble (or humiliated) enough to admit that he thought he might be crazy.[17] In Daven-port's time, the story of God mattered more than his pride. But ultimately, humble or not, his actions, among others, tainted how many viewed the Awakening. Many of those who sup-ported George Whitefield's revival were left embarrassed and confused. Those who despised Whitefield's "renewal" were de-lighted by Davenport's half-naked rip-and-snort through the public square. But Davenport survived, and despite his confessed insanity (and a Boston court agreeing with him), he lived to in-spire the world once more, moving to New Jersey, where he pastored a Presbyterian church until his death in 1757.

·   ·   ·

In the course of his thirty years in ministry, Whitefield preached eighteen thousand sermons, earned a multitude of American fans and followers of every race, creed, and religious affiliation, and played an influential role, though many believe unintentionally, in helping ripen America's desire for national liberty. Liberty was the main topic of his career, and the key word that ties his ministry to America's Revolution. Even though the liberty he spoke about was a spiritual liberty, few seemed capable, willing, or compelled to make any distinction between the liberty that Whitefield believed God offered individuals through new birth and the kind of national liberty that democracy and wars promote. According to Stephen Prothero, it makes sense that colonials didn't feel the need to disconnect spiritual liberty from national liberty. "People start to have a sense of ownership over their own experience," Prothero says. "They have experienced liberty. And this is the language Christians talk about, Christian freedom. They've had the experience of freedom, of being freed from sin."[18] To colonials, liberty was just that, liberty. Whether it was Christian or American, it was all a gift from God.

Many of Whitefield's chief supporters had no problem connecting God's liberty to America's story line. Thomas Kidd writes that "[the Great Awakening] stoked the belief of many Americans that religious signs portended major changes, including massive numbers of conversions, transformative political events, or both... [making them wonder] what the spiritual fervor might portend for the world at large."[19] In South Carolina, a friend of Whitefield's, the Reverend Josiah Smith, believed he knew. "Behold!... Some great things seem to be upon the anvil, some big prophecy at the birth; God give it strength to bring forth!"[20] And he was no doubt winking when he said that, because he knew, and those who heard him say it knew too, that he wasn't just talking about spiritual things. No, Reverend Smith, like many at the time, had turned his spiritual radar toward more political matters, a nationalized freedom in Christ, if you will. Nor was he alone. Many of Whitefield's fans, enthused with God's freedom—and with thoughts of a possible Constitution dancing in their heads—fully expected shake-ups, spiritual and political, to commence. And sometimes it was difficult to tell the two apart. Even Whitefield didn't make clear how exactly God differentiated personal freedom in Christ from national freedom.

In 1766, Whitefield republished a sermon he'd preached in response to the news that France was about to invade Great Britain. However, when published in the colonies, his words—"Our civil and religious Liberties are all, as it were, lying at Stake"—inspired new meaning. Whitefield believed that the true threat was not "France" but rather "Men of such corrupt mind" who have become careless with liberty.[21] Publicly, he mostly avoided playing spiritual politics.

Evident throughout his career, Whitefield's greatest passion was inviting people to God through Christ. But after his death in 1770, sparked by the opinions and stories of those who'd known him best, the line between his spirituality and his politics blurred. At his memorial service, one of Whitefield's closest friends, a Presbyterian minister named Nathaniel Whitaker, said, "[Whitefield] was a warm friend to religious liberty...[but] he was no less a friend to the civil liberties of mankind. He was a patriot, not in show, but reality, and an enemy to tyranny. He abhorred episcopal oppression....Thousands of happy souls here own him as the instrument in God's hand of their freedom from the insupportable tyranny of sin and Satan."[22]

Whitaker summed up rather nicely one of God's major American story lines, that patriotism would become an unofficial fruit of the Spirit, an American morality that sat next to godliness and often trumped tidings of great joy, peace, and overall goodwill toward other people.

. . .

In the years leading up to the signing of the Declaration of Independence, as the soon-to-be United States of America began to evolve out of its colonial state and into a less perfect union than what the Puritans imagined, so too did America's God evolve into the deity that best suited America's wants and needs. Though the evangelicals were on fire, a leftover spiritual fervor from the Awakening, some people thought that God was getting in the way of national progress.

It was a complicated time for God in America.

For starters, Americans were pulling God in different directions as they claimed with 100 percent certainty that they knew what kind of relationship God wanted to have with the future United States. The question that many Christians seemed most concerned with was how God and state would work together on an official basis. To a majority of Americans, there was nothing foreign about the concept of pushing God onto the populace. Many viewed the idea of putting God in bed with state as a way of offering God national credence. To them, including God in America's constitutional framework wasn't just a way of celebrating God; such an action would also, by law, protect God, protect America's values about God, and offer the state the opportunity not only to commemorate Christian orthodoxy but also to enforce that orthodoxy upon the country's citizens.

Though most of America's Christians loved the idea of including God in the nation's fundamental principles, a growing number of those same Christians had become vocal opponents of the state's enforcing one particular Christian orthodoxy over another. The evangelicals wanted God and America to work together without doctrinal fences or obligations. In other words, they didn't want America playing denominational favorites, enforcing Anglican dogma over Baptist dogma (or vice versa).

Surprisingly, each colony possessed laws of varying kinds marrying God to their governmental infrastructure. Some had formed Little Englands, as religion ruled in most. Even Rhode Island and Pennsylvania, colonies in which no official religion existed and religious tolerance was assumed, passed laws requiring "religious affiliation" as a prerequisite for serving in public office.

Benjamin Franklin fought against the inclusion of a religious litmus test in Pennsylvania. As he wrote in his *Autobiography*, he believed in "the existence of a deity, that [God] made the world, and governed it by his providence; that the most acceptable service of God was the doing good to man; that our souls are immortal; and that all crimes will be punished, and virtue rewarded either here or hereafter; these I esteemed the essentials of every religion."[23] Franklin wasn't sure what he thought about Jesus, but he professed certainty that God existed. However, he also believed in personal liberty. And he seemed quite distrustful of organized religion. "When a religion is good," Franklin wrote, "I conceive that it will support itself; and, when it cannot support itself, and God does not take care to support, so that its professors are obliged to call for the help of the civil power, it is a sign, I apprehend, of its being a bad one."[24] To Franklin's frustration, Pennsylvania passed the initiative, which required any officeholder to put his hand on a Bible and recite: *I do believe in one God, the creator and governor of the universe, the rewarder of the good and punisher of the wicked. And I do acknowledge the Scriptures of the Old and New Testament to be given by divine inspiration.*[25]

A battle between God and state and evangelicals had brewed in Virginia for several decades. In the beginning it was a mostly sermonic war of words, beliefs, and passions between the Anglicans (who were in charge) and the evangelicals (who were not). In 1743, evangelical Presbyterians from Pennsylvania and New

Jersey started doing missionary work in Virginia. The rector of St. Paul's Parish in Hanover, Virginia, Patrick Henry (the uncle of that other, more patriotic Patrick Henry), angrily condemned the Presbyterians, partly because of nasty rumors they were spreading about Anglicans throughout Virginia. According to the Presbyterians, the Anglicans weren't real Christians. Their sermons called into question the Anglicans' eternal salvation, suggesting that even the Reverend Henry was little more than a false teacher. In fact, according to the Presbyterians, the Anglicans were among the "Damn'd double damn'd ... Lumps of hellfire, incarnate Devils, 1000 times worse than Devils."[26] The Anglicans retaliated by imposing harsher regulations on those who preached a non-Anglican Gospel.

While the Presbyterians attempted to comply with Virginia's rules, the Baptists did not. The most vocal Baptist ministers were often beaten and sometimes imprisoned for not abiding by the Anglicans' laws. Jeremiah Moore, a Baptist from Fairfax County, Virginia, was in 1773 put in jail for preaching without a license. "I have," lamented Moore, "been told by the judge in his seat, 'You shall lie in jail until you rot,' when my crime was no other than preaching the gospel of Jesus Christ."[27] Crowds gathered outside Moore's cell, which only encouraged him to begin preaching his Gospel from behind bars.

Three years later, Moore brought a petition to Virginia's Assembly demanding "equal liberty" to preach the Gospel of his choosing. Ten thousand supporters signed the petition. One supporter of Moore's cause was Thomas Jefferson, who was then a member of the Assembly. Even though Jefferson was a professed Deist and thought the Baptists' teachings were outrageous, he believed in Moore's rights to teach them. So they joined forces, a union that led Jefferson to write a statute that would in effect lead the Assembly to disestablish the Anglican Church's rule in Virginia. The idea wasn't without opponents. Patrick Henry (the patriotic one) was a vocal adversary of disestablishment, suggesting that the last thing Virginia needed was to lose its religion. "The general diffusion of Christian knowledge," Henry wrote in his proposed bill, "hath a natural tendency to correct the morals of men, restrain their vices, and preserve the peace of society; which cannot be effected without a competent provision for learned teachers [pastors], who may be thereby enabled to devote their time and attention to the duty of instructing such citizens."

But Thomas Jefferson, in his presentation to the Assembly, gave 'em hell, which he seemed to believe might be supervised by Anglicans. "An individual cannot surrender [this] right—answerable to God," Jefferson claimed. "God requires every [religious] act according to belief, yet belief founded on the evidence offered to his mind, as things appear to him, not to another." And then, since Virginia's Anglicans had fashioned their laws according to British law, Jefferson said, "Is uniformity attainable? By inquisition. By lesser punishment—burnings heretics, fines, imprisoning, abjuration. Constraint may produce hypocrites, not prevent sentiment. Experience has proved unattainable—millions burnt, tortured, fined, imprisoned, yet men differ. In Roman Catholic countries, most infidelity."[28] Jefferson argued that "Liberty of conscience is the sacred property of every man." The bill that Virginia passed declared that *all men shall be free to profess and by argument to maintain their opinions in matters of religion.*

This was the first of many steps that Jefferson would take in order to secure "religious freedom" in America, a trend that would over time spread throughout the colonized America. Even though Jefferson rallied more for individual liberty than religious liberties, his work to disestablish the Anglican Church's control in his home state of Virginia started a movement. Soon other colonies would start the process of religious disestablishment in their states, a national shift that became one of the most influential outcomes of America's Revolution. Under Jefferson's guidance, the First Amendment would become an official part of the Constitution in 1791. As president, Jefferson would say, "Erecting the 'wall of separation between church and state,' therefore, is absolutely essential in a free society." Individual rights were protected. However, the repercussion of individual liberty was that God would become like a naked paper doll, one that free individuals could and would dress up into whatever Americanized deity they liked. Which is exactly what Americans have been doing with God all along, dressing him up in whatever divine (or secular) fashion we deem fitting, useful, sellable, or "true."

Contrary to the national trend, rather than fitting Jesus with religious and/or denominational garb, Jefferson, intoxicated by the Enlightenment and perhaps his role as president of the United States, decided to strip Jesus of his divine nature in an effort to magnify God's son's ethical wisdom. Working late at night, Jefferson began poring over the Bible's four Gospels, "abstracting what is really [Jesus's message] from the rubbish in which it is buried." The good stuff, according to Jefferson, was "easily distinguished by its lustre from the dross of his biographers, and as separate from that as the diamond from the dung hill."[29] Not completed until 1820, *The Jefferson Bible*, as it is called today, presents Jesus as a no-nonsense commonsense guy who taught people how to love, how to serve, and how to think, act, and live like Thomas Jefferson. In many ways, the Jesus that Jefferson fell in love with was, not so ironically, a lot like Jefferson, an enlightened Deist who, as Mark Noll describes, possessed a "faith in reason and commitment to liberty."[30]

Jefferson's Jesus, though he possessed a "benevolent heart" and an "enthusiastic mind," was also devoid of a virgin birth and a resurrection. Still, that hasn't prevented a large number of Christians from asking both Jesus and Thomas Jefferson into their hearts. The doctrines of Jefferson and Jesus would, as many historians and researchers suggest, collide once again years after Jefferson's death to play a significant role in shaping the mind-set of today's politically active Christian right. Darren T. Dochuk, author of *From Bible Belt to Sunbelt: Plain-Folk Religion, Grassroots Politics, and the Rise of Evangelical Conservatism*, believes the merging of "Jefferson and Jesus" formed a most holy ideological marriage that mixed nineteenth-century American populism with simple-minded American Christianity. Dochuk writes that this mind-set was rooted in Jefferson's philosophies about capitalism, freedom, power, "government by popular consensus," and, above all, "a commitment to the sanctity of the local community."[31] Those ideals, Dochuk suggests, "came wrapped in a package of Christian, plain-folk Americanism, an all-encompassing worldview that gave white southerners a sense of guardianship over their society."[32] The professor of humanities at the John C. Danforth Center on Religion and Politics believes this integration of Jefferson and Jesus is in many ways how members of the evangelical right can oppose abortion yet ignore the needs of disenfranchised members of society, how they can rage against sexual revolutions and offer little critique on economic greed or mass consumption, and how they can keep labor unions and government in check while not doing the same to Wall Street, insurance companies, and other big American businesses.

Of course, much of today's evangelical political doctrine has become so radical, so driven by fear and hyperbole that it's more or less a parody of the doctrines of Thomas Jefferson and Jesus, a culture where the poor in spirit are not blessed, they are marginalized and expected to care for themselves.

· · ·

Decades before Thomas Jefferson started editing Jesus, as the battle for religious freedom and individual liberty was brewing, the name of God was being used to support America's war for independence. The chief abuser was Patrick Henry, and in 1775 he used God's name in his now infamous cry for "liberty or death," an ultimatum he called "the great responsibility which we hold to God and country." According to Henry, the war against Great Britain was like a jihad, "[a] holy cause of liberty," ensuring that "we shall not fight our battles alone. There is a just God who presides over the destinies of Nations, and who will raise up friends to fight our battles for us." But broad-ranging support for military action against the British didn't materialize until the following year when Thomas Paine published his opinions in a pamphlet entitled *Common Sense*. Though Paine denied adhering to the beliefs of any church, whether Protestant or otherwise, and famously concluded that "my own mind is my own church," he wasn't beneath using God in a pinch. Much like the old Reverend Cotton of Puritan fame used biblical narrative to sell his New World dream, Paine used that same method in *Common Sense* to sell the Revolutionary War:

> Near three thousand years passed away from the Mosaic account of the creation, till the Jews under a national delusion requested a king. Till then their form of government (except in extraordinary cases, where the Almighty interposed) was a kind of republic administered by a judge and the elders of the tribes. Kings they had none and it was held sinful to acknowledge any being under that title but the Lord of Hosts. And when a man seriously reflects on the idolatrous homage which is paid to the persons of kings, he need not wonder that the Almighty, ever jealous of his honor, should disapprove of a form of government which so impiously invades the prerogative of heaven.[33]

Though Paine's personal value of scripture seemed pretty devoid of passion, trust, or even serious consideration, he understood fully the power it held over the Christianized mind. He knew that in order to build up support for the war against Great Britain, he needed to present a scripture-laced reasoning (references and all) to unite America's Christians, all of them, for this cause. And to Paine's credit, he constructed a masterful holy narrative. "We have it in our power to begin the world over again," he wrote. "A situation, similar to the present, hath not happened since the days of Noah until now. The birthday of a new world is at hand."[34] Paine played the role of a prophet—like the Prophet Samuel whose story he used to make his point—and convinced the American public that the "new world" was basically just like God's Ark, a huge vessel for which the rest of the world might be saved. But the Ark needed building! And it needed to be free. Under Paine's guidance, fighting Great Britain was not simply God's eternal destiny for the United States of America, it made "sense," because tea tax sucks!

At that point, Paine's personal understanding of God or the Bible or Christianity made little difference. He'd made God's point, at least as far as Americans were concerned. Suddenly, God in America was a pro-war deity who hated the redcoats, and this was true only because Paine—America's Prophet—said so. The following year, after the victory at Saratoga, Samuel Adams declared that it was "the indispensable duty of all men to adore the superintending providence of Almighty God; to acknowledge with gratitude their obligation to him for benefits received." Adams didn't stop there. He went on to say that God deserved gratitude "in the prosecution of a just and necessary war, for the defense and establishment of our unalienable rights and liberties."[35] Years later, as president of the United States, George Washington would offer these words in his inaugural address.

No people can be bound to acknowledge and adore the Invisible Hand which conducts the affairs of men more than
the people of the United States. Every step by which they
have advanced to the character of an independent nation
seems to have been distinguished by some token of prov-
idential agency....We ought to be no less persuaded that
the propitious smiles of Heaven can never be expected on
a nation that disregards the eternal rules of order and right
which Heaven itself has ordained.[36]

But Paine's words in 1776 would also set the tone for future
ideas to become spiritualized with biblical narrative, especially
how Christians today merge the stories of the children of Israel
with stories of the people of America. For example, author
Timothy Ballard believes Paine's words were "heaven sent." In
his book *The Covenant: America's Sacred and Immutable Connection to Ancient Israel*, Ballard begins one chapter with a
quote from *Common Sense*, the part where Paine associates
America's independence with the story of Noah in the Book
of Genesis. Which, ironically, might be where Paine makes the
least *Sense*. Nonetheless, for somebody like Ballard, an apologist
for "Christian America," Paine's American theologies serve as a
firm foundation for his *Covenant*. After quoting Paine, Ballard
writes:

God would inspire His new American settlers to turn
to their American Covenant, that He might pour upon
them the covenant blessings of liberty, protection, and
prosperity—those blessings required to ultimately secure
independence against all odds....Through it we can see
how, as the Founders worked to live according to their
obligations, the Lord continued providing the covenant
blessings that ultimately created an independent nation

whose hallmark would be an abundance of liberty unto a fullness of salvation.[37]

Since our nation's conception, there has always existed a very fine line between what is considered American and what is considered divine. While laws exist to help us manage the official relationship between America's church and America's state, those laws can't enforce how Americans think about God and country as well as blend country with God. (Have you seen the T-shirt printed with the word "JesUSAmerica"?) The common American belief before the Revolution was that to God, the United States of America was special. Many believed that God's love for this country was so great that he'd mapped out a heaven-designed "destiny" for us. This idea, of course, was birthed from John Winthrop's "city upon a hill" and from the Puritans' belief that they were God's "New Israel." After the Revolution, much of America became galvanized by pride, a national pride that was baptized in the assumption that America was divinely inspired, an integral part of God's ultimate plan for the world. Our destiny was in motion.

Garry Wills writes that "this [belief] would surface again in many guises—Manifest Destiny, American 'exceptionalism,' Ronald Reagan's invocation of Winthrop's 'City Upon a Hill,' the claim that we bring 'clean hands' to situations dirtied by European colonialism. This language is not derived solely from Puritans. But they sounded those notes loud and long, and the echoes had a long reverberation."[38]

. . .

America and God entered the nineteenth century not officially involved. The Constitution of the United States doesn't mention God, and for some Christians, that was a travesty. Leaving God's name out of the national details certainly affected the relationship between God and country, making their pairing more like a secret affair than a proper marriage.

In 1812, Congregationalist pastor Timothy Dwight, still in mourning over the godless state of the Constitution, wrote, "[It's] without any acknowledgement of God.... Thus we commenced our national existence, under the present system, without God."

With or without his name in the U.S. Constitution, God would continue to prosper in America. But not without challenges and change.

CHAPTER FIVE

THE INDEPENDENCE OF GOD

God in America is a free spirit, a supernatural entity capable of being shaped to fit a variety of ideas, Christian or otherwise. Like divine Play-Doh, America's God can be kneaded with hands, squashed between fingers, coerced into shapes, manipulated by devices, and, though it's not always recommended, digested by human bodies. Because God's Spirit is nontoxic. Or that was the original plan—that God's presence in our American lives would for the most part be a welcomed appearance or a spiritual companion never forced or contrived or mixed with artificial flavors. But slowly, in the effort to manifest the presence of God without waiting, Americans began fabricating God into products, consequently changing and shaping how the American people experienced God.

Branded "Bible-based" experiences with God are commonplace in today's fast-paced, message-drenched society. Unfortunately, Americans don't have time to wander around the wilderness for forty years and experience God for themselves, so it's much easier to attach our spiritual needs to the theologies and events of somebody else. That's why America fell in love with Pastor Rick Warren's *Purpose Driven Life*. The only Christian book to ever outsell the Bible nationally is Warren's easy-to-read and easy-to-understand biblical outline for how humans can discover God's divine purpose for their lives. After the huge success of *Purpose*, Warren's publisher, Zondervan, launched an all-out marketing extravaganza, including *40 Days of Purpose*, an evangelical Lenten-like season in which, rather than fasting, people gathered in groups and read Warren's book in the hope of discovering or rediscovering what God's purpose for their lives actually is or was. And Zondervan didn't stop there; they created *Purpose Driven* everything: plaques, day planners, journals, notepads, even clocks.

Capitalism has altered how Americans interact with the divine. For many of us, faith isn't the evidence of things unseen, it's the message printed on our doormats so people walking into our homes know what to expect. Under America's watch, God has been reduced to a commodity, a combination of ideas and products that we export, import, mass-produce, and display seasonally on our mantels. In today's evangelical culture, God sticks, clings, smells, burns, downloads, lights, ticks, and brightens dark corners.

Two hundred years ago, America's God wasn't nearly as multipurpose as he is today. He showed up in the most unexpected places and showcased his unique presence in unconventional ways. God didn't sit still or hang next to the toilet in their outhouses. America's God traveled.

· · ·

Throughout the nineteenth century, America's God was on the move. Following the American people westward over the Appalachians into places like Ohio, Kentucky, and Tennessee, God eventually made his way across the Mississippi and into the Wild West. No matter where Americans migrated, God went with them most of the time. Often, in the places where God settled down, revivals would break out. Usually instigated by one church or a group of churches, God showed up all the time, sometimes in the most curious places, and often spontaneously, sparked by a preacher whose messages seemed more inspired and angrier than the last minister who came through. But when God's Spirit showed up, people stopped, set up camp, and waited for the crowds to appear.

The most famous of these revivals was, as I mentioned in chapter one, the meeting that happened in Cane Ridge, Kentucky, in 1801. Though God's performance only lasted five or six days, that revival's effects set the temperature for what God would begin doing throughout America in the coming years. That spiritual gathering of mostly Methodists, Baptists, Presbyterians, and drunks—twenty-five thousand strong—morphed into what Harold Bloom calls an "American Orphism." Regarding the events at Cane Ridge, Bloom writes, "denominational differences dissolved," allowing the attendees to become "rapt by ecstasy."[1]

Barton Stone, a Presbyterian minister from Maryland, was one of the preachers who got caught up in the rhapsody of God's Spirit over the course of that week. The spiritual craving that Stone experienced led him to leave the Presbyterian Church and ultimately find his roots in the foundations of what would become the Church of Christ and Christian Church (also called Disciples of Christ). Bloom believes that "Stone preached at Cane Ridge not as a prophet of future denominations . . . but primarily as a fugitive from Calvinism." That might be an exaggeration to some degree, but Stone's experience at Cane Ridge indeed led him to become a raging critic of Calvinism, his onetime theological home. About his former theology, Stone wrote:

Calvinism is among the heaviest clogs on Christianity in the world. It is a dark mountain between heaven and earth, and is among the most discouraging hindrances to sinners from seeking the kingdom of God, and engenders bondage and gloominess to the saints. Its influence is felt throughout the Christian world, even where it is least suspected. Its first link is total depravity. Yet are there thousands of precious saints in this system.[2]

Stone's reflections about Calvinism showcase one of the most influential outcomes of America's Second Great Awakening: America's broad-ranging dismissal of John Calvin's version of God. Another vocal (and potentially insane) critic of Reformed doctrine was itinerant preacher Charles Grandison Finney. Like Stone, Finney left his Presbyterian roots after experiencing "a mighty baptism of the Holy Ghost," which he claimed felt "like a wave of electricity going through and through," a shock that "seemed to come in waves of liquid love."[3] Finney's "Jesus experience" was life-changing, an event that led him to leave his profession as a lawyer and become an evangelist. In fact, the morning after his conversion, he told one of his clients, "I have a retainer from the Lord Jesus Christ to plead his cause and I cannot plead yours."

Years later, in 1830, Finney preached at Third Presbyterian Church in Rochester, New York, to a congregation made up of merchants and craftsmen, most of whom had Calvinism running through their veins, doctrinal chromosomes genetically passed down to them by their parents and their parents' parents. They worshiped a God who "foreordained whatsoever comes to pass," and believed that man "could alter neither their individual spiritual states nor shape their societies."[4] Despite their staunch Reformed heritage, they'd also heard the rumors about the revivals being led by preachers whose missions were to dismantle their theological worldview.

Finney was one of the loudest critics; he'd been fighting

against the evils of Calvinism since the 1820s and was quite accustomed to speaking in front of ornery pro-Reformed audiences. But as vile as he believed Calvinism to be, his understanding of God wasn't exactly cute and cuddly. For example, Finney believed that "[the sinner] must be condemned; he must incur the penalty of the law of God." A strict advocate for human perfection and quite possibly the father of American fundamentalism, Finney possessed an odd (and rather cruel) comprehension of God, one whose perspectives on "the free will of man" were as much a crime against humanity as those that Calvinists preached. Nevertheless, his words lit up the ears of those in attendance at Third Presbyterian, as he shouted that "God has made man a moral free agent," an idea that undermined that Rochester congregation's entire doctrine of predestination. According to the notes by one of the revival's attendees, Finney said that if all of the world's Christians united under one cause, they could "convert the world and bring on the millennium in three months time."[5]

Even though Finney's message was, at its core, biblically based individualism—a faith that was centered fully on a human's ability or willingness to choose to believe—the crowd that day practically leaped out of their pews to join his evangelical assault. In the months following Finney's appearance, the folks of Rochester's Third Presbyterian helped to wage a regional spiritual war, one that led to a multitude of conversions in their communities. The revivals were so potent that Lyman Beecher, an evangelical contemporary of Finney's and one of the most influential revivalists of the Second Great Awakening, declared that Finney's work in Rochester "was the greatest work of God, and the greatest revival of religion, that the world has ever seen."

Modern opinions on Finney's influence vary from praise (Jerry Falwell called him his "hero" and implied that without Finney there would be no Billy Graham) to abhorrence (Dr.

Michael Horton, professor of systematic theology and apologetics at Westminster Seminary California, writes, "No single man is more responsible for the distortion of Christian truth in our age than Charles Grandison Finney").[6] Those strong opinions aside, Finney's war against Reformed theology played a key role in the fall of Calvinism. "No doctrine," Finney declared, "is more dangerous than this to the prosperity of the Church, and nothing more absurd."

Calvinism had a plethora of critics other than Stone and Finney, including the famous Methodist John Wesley. Wesley said that "unconditional election"—one of the tenets of Calvinism—made his blood boil. And not surprisingly, Thomas Jefferson despised Calvinism too; in a letter to John Adams, Jefferson lamented:

I can never join Calvin in addressing his god. He was indeed an Atheist, which I can never be; or rather his religion was Daemonism. If ever man worshipped a false god, he did. The being described in his 5. points is not the God whom you and I acknowledge and adore, the Creator and benevolent governor of the world; but a daemon of malignant spirit. It would be more pardonable to believe in no god at all, than to blaspheme him by the atrocious attributes of Calvin. Indeed I think that every Christian sect gives a great handle to Atheism by their general dogma that, without a revelation, there would not be sufficient proof of the being of a god. Now one sixth of mankind only are supposed to be Christians: the other five sixths then, who do not believe in the Jewish and Christian revelation, are without a knowledge of the existence of a god![7]

. . .

The Second Great Awakening altered much about God, Christianity, and how people expressed and interacted with the divine. As rumors of the revivals spread, the news sparked awakenings all across the United States, from Georgia and the Carolinas to New York, Pennsylvania, the Mid-Atlantic states, and throughout New England. Seemingly, God was growing accustomed to the rugged, less frilly American way of life. Gone were the days of God being locked up inside stuffy Boston seminaries or legislated by Anglican elitists in Richmond. Technically, God still existed in Massachusetts and Virginia, but his Spirit seemed to prefer the freedom of adventure, pioneering, and uncertainty.

God in America was diversifying. Congregational and Anglican churches remained a dominating force in the decade or two following the Revolution, but their growth had stalled and their leadership had become paralyzed by intellectualism. In the new century, as the Second Great Awakening surged and Americans thirsted for God and spirituality, God began joining various evangelical sects, groups that gathered together based on the attributes of God they believed and the doctrines they adhered to. God mingled with the Baptists—all kinds of Baptists—from Free Will Baptists to Primitive Baptists. God became a Disciple of Christ. God dwelt among Presbyterians and Lutherans. For many, God was a Christ-centered Universalist. And then suddenly, God stopped being a Christ-centered Universalist. To some, God was a Latter-day Saint, and eventually, to others, God became a Seventh-day Adventist.

But by far, as God's interest in Congregationalism and Anglicanism faded and the Second Awakening opened the spiritual eyes of Americans, the Christian sect that God worked alongside the most was the Methodists. Mark Noll believes that the Second Great Awakening was all about the Methodists: "The religious wonders of the age were the more aggressively evangelical churches—Presbyterians advancing at or slightly above the rate of the general population growth, Baptists and the new Disciples /Christian Churches far above, and the Methodists off the chart in a class all of their own."[8] Methodism soared during the first half of the nineteenth century. From 1800 to 1860, America's Methodist churches swelled in membership from 65,000 to 1,744,000.[9] "By the 1850s the Methodists by themselves—joined together through an interlocking system of personal and epistolary contact—had constructed almost as many churches as there were post offices and employed almost as many ministers as there were postal workers."[10]

America's Methodist fever in the nineteenth century was a core reason for the decline of Calvinism in the United States. Baptists were the other reason. The Methodists and the Baptists adhered to another theology altogether. A small number of Calvinist-leaning congregations existed within the Methodist and Baptist denominations—though most of these congregations believed in a modified form of John Calvin's God—but the majority of Methodists and Baptists followed some variation of the Arminian theology developed by Dutch Reformer Jacobus Arminius, a onetime devout Calvinist who began having doubts about Reformed doctrine after a careful study of the Book of Romans. Arminius's conclusions led him to construct a theology of his own, a study of God that promoted spiritual ideas like an atonement that was unlimited, a divine grace that was resistible by humans, and that humans, though capable of resisting sin, could indeed fall from God's grace.

However, Arminius's most discussed point is his belief in the free will of humanity. Rather than adhering to the belief that God preordains the eternal salvation of an individual before birth (and being quite particular about who gets chosen), an Arminian believes that God's eternal salvation is a gift, one that people can either accept or reject. But Arminius's guiding principle for outlining his view of God wasn't about the free will of people as much as it was his belief that God is good, that God's goodness not only manages God's power, it is inseparable from his glory. Furthermore, one of Arminius's chief intentions was to avoid making God the author of sin.[11]

Scholars on both sides of the Arminian versus Calvinism debate (as well as those who sit somewhere in the middle) will debate, differentiate, compare, and ridicule one side or both until Kingdom Come. Fine, let them, but the significant difference between these two ideas, the stuff affecting the faiths of everyday people, is this: One side cannot fathom a God who cherry-picks souls that will go to heaven and souls that will go to hell, and the other side believes that God's sovereignty over the eternal destinies of humanity (divine cherry-picking) only magnifies his glory, power, and honor.

For Methodist preachers like Peter Cartwright, one of the nineteenth century's most well-traveled circuit-riding preachers, the Calvinism vs. Arminian debate wasn't nearly as complicated as many throughout history had made it. To Cartwright, believing in Calvinism was just another reason to get down on your knees and confess. Once, while he was preaching at the funeral of a man called Brother L, the sad occasion attracted a large audience of Calvinists from the local Baptist church. Remembering this event, Cartwright wrote, "A great many of their members gave up Calvinism, closed communion and immersion, and joined the Methodist Church; and we took possession of their meeting-house, and raised a large society there that flourishes to this day."[12]

Cartwright converted a multitude of Calvinists during his many rounds. He seemed to take the challenge almost as sport, often purposefully preaching his God in front of Calvinists to see how many he could win over. At one such meeting, at First Congregational Church in Marietta, Ohio, Cartwright wrote, "I was treated with great respect by the Congregational minister and his people, and the Academy....I begged the privilege to make one more appointment in the Academy...[and] as it was only one more time, was granted. I then prepared myself; and when my appointed day rolled around, the house was crowded; and I leveled my whole Arminian artillery against their Calvinism....This effort secured me many friends, and some persecution."[13]

This was how the Methodists changed America's God from a Calvinist to an Arminian—by sending traveling preachers like Peter Cartwright out on five- to six-week missional rounds. In 1784, the Methodist Church employed only eighty-three circuit riders; by 1839, the most influential denomination in America boasted 3,557 traveling preachers and 5,856 local. Cartwright defined the Methodists' success like this:

The Presbyterians and other Calvinistic branches of the Protestant Church used to contend for an educated ministry, for pews, for instrumental music, for a congregational or state salaried ministry. The Methodists universally opposed these ideas; and the illiterate Methodist preachers actually set the world on fire (the American world at least) while they were lighting their matches.[14]

The reason the God of the Methodists became America's God during the Second Great Awakening was because of Jesus. Now, I don't mean "Jesus" in the syrupy spiritual way that evangelicals sometimes mean "Jesus." Along with a number of Baptist churches, the Methodists' enjoyed success during the early years of the nineteenth century because, rather than focusing on heavy-handed theologizing, hyper-focusing on the organizational structures of the church, or attempting to overcontrol people's lifestyles through politics and social strictures, they made Jesus the alpha and omega of their Gospel message.

Stephen Prothero writes that "covenant theology took its cues from Israel more than Galilee, focusing not on the individual's relationship with God the Son but on the community's covenant with God the Father. . . . The Puritans, in short, were a God-fearing rather than a Jesus-loving people."[15] Even though George Whitefield and others like him began mentioning Jesus more in the eighteenth century, many of America's Christians struggled with what to do with Jesus. They'd never heard that Jesus was homeless and looking for a place to live inside our bodies' circulatory systems. Some doctors at the time were still draining sick people of their blood, sucking them dry of life, because they believed that the blood was killing them. So the idea that Jesus would inhabit the human body in any fashion wouldn't begin to become a part of the Christian conversation until much later. Prior to the Methodists and Baptists going on an all-out evangelical crusade against the forces of evil—drunkenness, laziness, and Calvinism—America's Christians didn't pursue relationships with Jesus.

Furthermore, and crucial to the narrative of God in America, when Jesus did get mentioned, it was most often in reference to his divinity and not his humanity. At the time, Americans did not contemplate Jesus's humanness. They did not understand how it might help them connect more deeply with God. America's interest in the humanity of Jesus was triggered, in part, by Thomas Jefferson's obsession with the morality and values of Jesus.

Francis Asbury, a minister who migrated from Great Britain, helped to launch Jesus's American fame. In 1784, he wrote a plan that became the official model for how Methodism in America would be accomplished:

> Our grand plan, in all its parts, leads to an itinerant ministry. Our bishops are traveling bishops. All the different order which compose our conferences are employed in the

THE INDEPENDENCE OF GOD

traveling line; and our local preachers are, in some degree, traveling preachers. Everything is kept moving as far as possible; and we will be bold to say that, next to the grace of God, there is nothing like this for keeping the whole body alive from the center to the circumference; and for the continual extension of that circumference on every hand.[16]

The Methodist message was, as Asbury put it, the exact message that the Apostle Paul wrote to the church of Corinth: "I determined not to know anything among you save Jesus Christ, and him crucified." That simple message became the framework of American Methodism—*Jesus died for your sins!*—a message that for the next seventy years would be delivered to the masses with fanatical enthusiasm by a band of horse-riding Bible thumpers. Asbury's model for evangelism worked. By the eve of the Civil War, Methodism was the largest Protestant denomination in the United States. In the decades to follow, it would lead the most enterprising world missionary campaign of the nineteenth century. No other denomination has affected the basic structure of American Christianity more than the Methodist Church. Its influence on America's God is immeasurable. That's what David Hempton believes, anyway. In his book about Methodism, the dean of Harvard's divinity school writes:

By the end of the nineteenth century a new and formidable empire of the spirit had come into existence. Moreover, if one takes seriously the recent work of historians and sociologists who argue that the explosion of Pentecostalism in the twentieth century (ironically just taking off when Methodism's New History appeared) can best be explained as a much-modified continuation of the Methodist holiness tradition, then at least another 250 million religious enthusiasts could be added to the statistical heap. The speed of

Pentecostal growth in Africa, South America, and Asia is staggering. Philip Jenkins states, "According to current projections, the number of Pentecostal believers should surpass the one billion mark before 2050."[17]

. . .

If the Puritans brought God to America, it was the Methodists who freed God from the theological clutches of Calvinist theology and refocused America's faith onto God, the Son, rather than God, the Father. The Methodists, with help from the Baptists, laid the spiritual foundation for American Christianity to develop into a faith that would become riddled with individualism, politics, and parapsychological activity. Christian celebrities like Rick Warren, Billy Graham, Pat Robertson, and others would likely not exist without the stronghold of the Methodist ideology of the nineteenth century. The messages of the Methodist Church helped to connect Jesus to the individual American, making God's son more accessible and more important to their everyday lives than ever before.

Historian Gregory Schneider believes that the core of Methodist spiritualism was something he calls "the mystery of intimacy," a faith that Mark Noll says opposed formality but insisted that outward behavior showcase the heart's conversion.[18] Noll also suggests that the intimacy with Jesus the Methodists sought is reflected in the lyrics of this 1856 hymn:

> *I thirst, thou wounded Lamb of God,*
> *To wash me in thy cleansing blood;*
> *To dwell within thy wounds; then pain*
> *Is sweet, and life or death is gain.*
> *Take my poor heart, and let it be*
> *For ever clos'd to all but thee!*

Seal thou my breast, and let me wear
That pledge of love for ever there.
How blest are they who still abide
Close shelter'd in thy bleeding side!
Who life and strength from thence derive,
And by thee move, and in thee live.
What are our works but sin and death,
Till thou thy quick'ning Spirit breathe?
Thou giv'st the power thy grace to move;
O wond'rous grace! O boundless love![19]

A new kind of Christian spirituality was beginning to take shape in America, a mystical celebration of God not stifled by intellectualism and rigid theologies but rather dependent upon an individual's emotional, mental, and physical relationship with Jesus Christ.

CHAPTER SIX

THE DIVIDED STATES OF GOD

God was in Houston in 2013. Numerous members of the Southern Baptist Convention (SBC) sent God the request to *pleeeeeeeeaaaaase* show up. It was June, and each June thousands of Southern Baptists gather in a city for their annual denominational meeting. God was already planning to be at the SBC meet-and-greet. God's been putting SBC-sponsored events on his calendar since 1845. That was the year a group of disgruntled Baptist ministers—godly men who loved slavery—met in Augusta, Georgia, and formed the SBC. According to many, God's been hanging out with Southern Baptists ever since. At their weddings, during their funerals, in their Baptistry tanks, and whenever two or more people are gathered together in Birmingham, Alabama, God is there.

It was crucial that God show up at the SBC's gathering in Houston, because the Southern Baptists were under attack. That wasn't a huge surprise, really. At any given moment, most Southern Baptists will tell you that Southern Baptists are under attack. Their paranoia is somewhat warranted, I suppose. As America's largest (and often most vocal) Protestant denomination, Southern Baptists have become one of the media's favorite punching bags. And while the SBC often brings the media's wrath upon itself—that eight-year boycott of Disney, for starters—one does have to wonder at what point does "Southern Baptists acting like Southern Baptists" stop being news?

That said, the media's interest in the SBC's activities in Houston was justified. Lots of people, Christians and otherwise, were tuned in to the SBC's convention that year. Every major news outlet in the country was stuffed inside a liquorless press room in Houston; they were waiting (practically salivating) to tell the world about the events happening inside the George R. Brown Convention Center.

The media was present for the same reason Southern Baptists needed God to show up, because the Boy Scouts of America (BSA) had decided to stop excluding gay kids from being Boy Scout members. Earlier that year, the Boy Scouts' fourteen hundred voting members "approved a resolution to remove the restriction denying membership to youth on the basis of sexual orientation alone." Not surprising, some Southern Baptists were irate. Tim Reed, pastor of a Baptist church in Arkansas, told CNN, "God's word explicitly says homosexuality is a choice, a sin." Pastor Reed swore his opinions had nothing to do with hate. "It's not a hate thing here. It's a moral stance we must take as a Southern Baptist church." Wes Taylor, a Southern Baptist pastor from California, wasn't happy either. He told the *Los Angeles Times*, "Homosexuality is directly opposed to everything that Scouting stands for.... [The BSA is] moving away from the principles that it was founded upon. It is an environment that would prove just fertile for young boys to be exposed to something that is ungodly and unacceptable."[1]

The SBC needed God to be in Houston because they needed "divine intervention," which is what Christians say when they actually mean "crisis management."

According to Frank Page, the SBC's executive committee president, "God showed up."[2] That's what he told the enthusiastic crowd of Southern Baptist messengers. And what did God do? God helped the SBC form a resolution, one that didn't involve an all-out boycott of the BSA but instead put the power to choose "gay or nay" in the hands of individual churches. In other words, individual churches were given the power to choose whether or not they would continue to allow their local Boy Scout troops to utilize their facilities for meetings. The SBC's plan also included their intentions to render unto the BSA a firm scolding from God.

The SBC issued to the BSA an official memo voicing their "disappointment" and reminding them what they believed God thought about homosexuality. The SBC's memo also said that "[their membership policy] has the potential to complicate basic understandings of male friendships, needlessly politicize human sexuality, and heighten sexual tensions within the Boy Scouts."[3]

Two days later, SBC's president, Fred Luter, told Alabama's AL.com that his own Baptist church in New Orleans would be "pulling out of Boy Scouts." His unfortunate choice of words aside, Luter noted that he wasn't at all surprised that the SBC had voted to take a stand against the BSA. "We believe in the Bible," he said.[4]

Therein lies the key to some of America's biggest social divisions: the Bible. How a Christian views and understands the Bible will dictate not only his or her worldview but, more importantly, how they interact with the worldviews of other people. America's Christians have long used the Bible to wield power, influence, justification, and control, and it's often used as a "good excuse" to hate, bully, or limit the rights of somebody who dares to disagree with them. Using the Bible as a double-edged sword, Americans have, in many cases, divided God into multiple identities. The Bible is the root cause of the deep divisions that separate America's faithful. Why else would America's churches have so many different ideas about God, ideas based on what we believe God thinks and/or feels about a number of topics, from issues regarding modesty and feminism to atonement and eschatology to drumbeats, spiritual gifts, hair length, masculinity, social justice, and sexuality? The list of ways in which we have divided God into denominational, theological, and cultural pieces is endless.

But much of America's big God isn't about God at all; it's about the Bible. For many Christians, the Bible *is* God—the Word in Flesh, translated into English, and printed on pretty paper. And while a Bible-sized God is easy to fit inside purses or tuck beneath armpits, it can also make human relationships with others more difficult, turn regular Joes into pontificating biblical elitists, and make everyday normal molehills into mountains of biblical proportions. Bible-sized God offers people "holy" excuses to rage against other groups. Throughout our *Christianish* history, Americans have used scripture to marginalize, manipulate, violate, excuse, and disregard other people.

Fred Luter was right. Southern Baptists do believe in the Bible. In fact, Southern Baptists have a long history of using the Bible as an excuse to be, well, Southern Baptists.

· · ·

In the 1840s, God was a slave owner. In fact, God had been championing slavery in America almost from the beginning. America's pro-slave-owning God was, by most people's accounts, the same God who'd spent the last forty-some years manifesting spiritual havoc in America, giving people the Holy Ghost shakes, slaying them prostrate, paralyzing their bodies, and slowly molding America into one nation under himself.

Believing that God was a proponent of slavery made sense to many Christians at the time. After all, owning slaves was addressed in the Bible as a functioning part of everyday society. In the Book of Titus, chapter two, the Apostle Paul wrote: *Exhort servants to be obedient unto their own masters, and to please them well in all things*. Paul also addressed "servants" in the Book of Ephesians, chapter six: *Servants, be obedient to them that are your masters according to the flesh, with fear and trembling, in singleness of your heart, as unto Christ*. Like the majority of America's Christians, fans of slavery cherry-picked the parts of the Bible that worked best with their lifestyle.

Besides having the support of the holy scriptures, slave owners also had the support of some of America's best-known Christian saints. How could you argue against the spiritual logic of Jonathan Edwards, the great Calvinist orator who was famous for promoting God's passion for roasting souls over hellfire? In spite of his "glory," Edwards's dirty well-known secret was that he owned slaves. Though his son, Jon Jr., eventually joined the abolitionist movement, Edwards himself remained a slave owner until he died in 1758.

Another proponent for slavery was George Whitefield. In addition to lobbying on behalf of slavery in his favored state of Georgia, he was known for trying to rectify his potentially guilty conscience by looking for contextual possibilities (or lame excuses) within the biblical narrative. In a letter to a friend from Great Britain, Whitefield wrote:

As for the lawfulness of keeping slaves, I have no doubt, since I hear of some that were bought with Abraham's money, and some that were born in his house. And I cannot help thinking, that some of those servants mentioned by the Apostles in their epistles, were or had been slaves. It is plain, that the Gibeonites were doomed to perpetual slavery, and though liberty is a sweet thing to such as are born free, yet to those who never knew the sweets of it, slavery perhaps may not be so irksome.[5]

However, the grossest and most ludicrous way in which Whitefield spiritually condoned slavery was by celebrating how many of his own slaves experienced "new birth." Later in the same letter he wrote, "It rejoiced my soul, to hear that one of my poor negroes in Carolina was made a brother in Christ."[6] Whitefield often wrote or spoke about the evangelism of slaves as if "hearing the Gospel" made being owned all better.

But America's most famous Christian slave owner was Patrick Henry. In a letter to his friend John Alsop, a Quaker and pro-abolitionist, the man who would two years later beg for liberty or death confessed his hypocrisy regarding owning slaves:

Would any one believe that I am master of slaves by my own purchase? I am drawn along by the general inconvenience of living without them. I will not—I cannot justify it, however culpable my conduct....I believe a time will come when an opportunity will be afforded to abolish this lamentable evil. Everything we can do, is to improve it, if it happens in our day; if not, let us transmit to our descendants, together with our slaves, a pity for their unhappy lot, and an abhorrence of Slavery. If we cannot reduce this wished-for reformation to practice, let us treat the unhappy victims with lenity. It is the furthest advancement we can make toward justice. It is a debt we owe to the purity of our religion, to show that it is at variance with that law which warrants Slavery.[7]

Now, despite the large number of Christian leaders who supported slavery as holy, it did have a host of Christian enemies too, those who waged, on God's behalf, a war against the owning and trading of slaves. Initially, slavery's chief opponents were mostly Quakers. Many Methodists fought against it too, including John Wesley and Francis Asbury. They spoke vehemently against the vile actions of one man owning another. But in the days before America's Revolution, the odds were stacked high against the voices that supported abolition and racial equality.

. . .

By the middle of the Second Great Awakening, it appeared that God might be changing his mind about slavery, from a legal standpoint anyway. The international slave trade had been made illegal in the United States, which allowed Christians to become more active in their fight for abolition.

The Presbyterians were one of the first denominations to disown slavery officially. In 1818, when they gathered for their General Assembly, their representatives voted boldly and unanimously to denounce the institution, declaring it "a gross violation of the most precious and sacred rights of human nature" and "utterly inconsistent with the law of God" and "with the spirit and the principles of the Gospel of Christ."[8]

The general assumption among Americans at the time was that making slavery illegal was the way culture was moving. However, in 1820, the Missouri Compromise tossed a wrench into the antislavery movement and motivated proslavery initiatives in the South.[9] Fifteen years passed, and in that time the American climate—the North versus the South—began to change, an ideology that began inside the walls of the church. Peter Cartwright blamed his own spiritual kind, the Methodists. Cartwright said that Methodist ministers "preached loudly against [slavery]" because they couldn't afford to participate. But then their financial circumstances changed. Some got married. Some started making money. That was when they started to "apologize for the evil; then to justify it on legal principles;

then on Bible principles—till lo and behold!—it is not an evil but a good! It is not a curse but a blessing!" Known for using satire to embellish his point, Cartwright concluded that eventually Methodist preachers implied that "you would go to the Devil for not enjoying the labor, toil, sweat of this degraded race—and all this without rendering them any equivalent whatever!"[10]

But it wasn't only Methodists who apologized for slavery. Samuel B. How, a Dutch Reformer from New Jersey, preached that "[the Bible teaches] that there are rights of property; that there are masters and that there are slaves, and bids us to respect the rights of the master, and not to covet his man-servant or his maid-servant." And Richard Furman, a Baptist, explained that the "right of holding slaves is clearly established in the Holy Scriptures, both by precept and example."[11]

. . .

During the two decades preceding the Civil War, the war over what God believed to be true about slavery raged inside America's churches. Ironically, the denominations most divided over the issue were the same ones that experienced the most growth during the Second Awakening. Garry Wills writes, "A great blow ran like some historic cleaver through the Presbyterian, Methodist, and Baptist communities, dividing the country—religiously—into two nations."[12]

Two nations under two Gods wasn't the plan. But that was how it was starting to look by the late 1830s, like the Tale of Two Cities Upon a Hill. The first schism happened to the Presbyterians, one that started at the denomination's assembly in 1837 and didn't fully complete its divide until almost twenty years later. The two sides fought a nasty battle over slavery, each mixing God into their reasons for or against people being property. Two groups existed in the Presbyterian Church, God's Old

School Presbyterians and God's New School Presbyterians. Old Schools were the more popular group, more Calvinistic, more southern, and the general sentiment was *more slaves, please.* New Schools were growing but not as large nor as organized as their Old counterparts. The New Presbyterians were located in the North, leaned theologically liberal, and were aiding abolitionists.

In 1837, the General Assembly cleared its ranks of all New School members and declared a ban on any pronouncements against slavery. After its official split in 1857, the Presbyterian Church's presence in the South dwindled and its growth flourished in the North and West.

The Methodists divided too. As abolitionism became more popular among the Methodist Church and congregations felt brave enough to join the cause, the biblical gap between northern and southern Methodists widened. In 1836, fed up with the antislavery heresy seeping into his denomination, South Carolina's bishop, William Capers, charged abolitionists as carriers of "a false philosophy, overreaching and setting aside the Scriptures." Capers called the antislavery revolution "utterly erroneous." But the abolitionary Methodists refused to be silenced. In 1843, Methodists held an antislavery gathering in Boston. The meeting unified their message against slavery, calling it "a flagrant violation of the law of God." The back-and-forth rhetoric only grew in intensity. Both sides, armed with Bible verses, raged against each other until America's largest denomination could no longer remain unified under one version of God, let alone one denomination. In 1844, the Methodists split. The two sides remained apart until 1939.

America's Baptists were the least organized of the three denominations. While Baptist churches had come together under one entity in 1814, there was no grandiose deacon board telling the churches what they could and could not do. Each church managed its congregation as an independent ministerial unit. The only unified associations within the Baptist denomination were two mission boards, one group that oversaw foreign missions and one that oversaw home missions. Discord started when the mission boards started denying "missionary status" to young preachers who owned slaves. When Georgia Baptists nominated James Reeves, a slave owner, to be a missionary to Indians, the Home Mission Society said no. The Baptists in Georgia grew irate because they wanted their slave-owning missionary to win native souls for Jesus. The following year, all of the congregations in Georgia that loved slavery gathered in Augusta in 1845 and decided to form their own denomination, the Southern Baptist Convention. In 1995, 150 years after that meeting in Georgia, Southern Baptist leaders finally issued an official press release renouncing the SBC's stance on slavery and segregation and offering a formal apology.

· · ·

In *Uncle Tom's Cabin*, author Harriet Beecher Stowe wrote, "A day of grace is yet held out to us...and the *Christian church* has a heavy account to answer." The book was published in 1852, just as the battle over slavery between God and churches was beginning to boil over. Stowe's strong message to America's church was directed at both northern and southern Christians. Stowe feared that God's wrath was growing close and that God's grace was wearing thin. Stowe believed the only remedies were "repentance, justice and mercy":

A day of grace is yet held out to us. Both North and South have been guilty before God; and the *Christian church* has a heavy account to answer. Not by combining together, to protect injustice and cruelty, and making a common capital of sin, is this Union to be saved,—but by repentance, justice and mercy; for, not surer is the eternal law by which the millstone sinks in the ocean, than that stronger law, by which injustice and cruelty shall bring on nations the wrath of Almighty God![13]

Even though Stowe's sentiment was well grounded in the popular theology of her time, America's religious were far too busy working their own agendas to stop and repent. God was on each of their sides, according to the Bible.

God was no spectator to this religious clash. Neither was he a middleman working to form a mutual agreement between slavery and freedom. America's God was a grand participant, a reason to fight for equality, and an excuse to fight for the right to own slaves. God aided both sides. Leading up to the Civil War, America's God was a two-faced deity working with both the North and the South.

God was for slavery.

And God was against slavery.

God's name was praised among the slaves.

And God's name was praised among the owners of slaves.

God was pro-equality.

And God was a complete and utter racist.

God helped preachers and politicians in the South form messages and rhetoric that suggested slavery was good.

And God helped countless slaves find passageways toward freedom.

Not even God, with help from Abraham Lincoln, could stop the pandemonium that would begin in 1861, the bloodiest conflict in American history, the Civil War.

. . .

When the Civil War ended in April 1865, the relationship between God and America was strained. The war had sucked the soul out of the nation. Few families were unaffected. Americans on both sides were happy to see an end to the fighting and chaos, and Edward Beecher was one of them. The abolitionist preacher, brother of Harriet Beecher Stowe, was ecstatic, proclaiming, "Now that God has smitten slavery unto death, he has opened the way for the redemption of [America's] whole social system."[14]

Maybe Beecher was right; maybe God's perfect plan for America did include a section on how to redeem America's social order after the Civil War. But if God did have such a plan, it either wasn't working or proved too difficult, even for God.

Few people knew exactly what God was thinking at the time. Whether God was rejoicing or mourning depended largely on whom you talked to, where they were from, and what church they attended.

Pastors across New England offered thanksgiving unto God. "We thank Thee for the triumph of right over wrong," was what Boston's Phillips Brooks prayed. "We thank Thee for the loyal soldiers planted in the streets of wickedness.... And now, O God, we pray Thee to complete Thy work." According to Brooks, the Union army was made up of pure and righteous men, like missionaries holding muskets rather than Bibles, ridding God's country of evildoers. But that wasn't just Brooks's idea, that was how most of the North understood the Civil War. On one hand they knew it was a war about freeing slaves, but on the other, they also believed it was a war about advancing God's Kingdom.

Historian George Marsden put the Union's perspective like this: "When [Northerners] sang, 'Mine eyes have seen the glory of the coming of the Lord,' their thoughts were not far from the victories of General Sherman or General Grant." At the time, most Christians on either side of the border states believed that their work on earth was to create a nation made up of Christian citizenship. Marsden writes that "American Protestants at midcentury [1850s] frequently had proclaimed that a Christian millennium was not far away."[15]

For Christians in the North, slavery posed a threat to God's national purpose for America. God wasn't going to bless a nation that harbored slave owners. So for many the Civil War was a spiritual war, a war of "unseen things," as much as it was a war between flesh and blood. Among black Americans, both free and enslaved, spiritualizing their plight was a common theme in the songs they sung. Much as the Puritans borrowed biblical narratives to sell God's vision for heading to the "Promise Land" in Boston, the slaves used biblical imagery—Pharaoh versus Israel, Jesus versus the devil, and Good versus Evil—to cast hope and light into the darkness of their circumstances. President Lincoln spiritualized America's Civil War too, calling it God's wrath on America for engaging in two-hundred-plus years of slavery. Lincoln deepened the connection between God and America's ordeal during his second inaugural address:

Both [the North and South] read the same Bible and pray to the same God, and each invokes His aid against the other.... The Almighty has His own purposes. "Woe unto the world because of offenses; for it must needs be that offenses come, but woe to that man by whom the offense cometh." If we shall suppose that American slavery is one of those offenses which, in the providence of God, must needs come, but which, having continued through His appointed time, He now wills to remove, and that He gives to both North and South this terrible war as the woe due to those by whom the offense came, shall we discern therein any departure from those divine attributes which the believers in a living God always ascribe to Him?[16]

Though technically, America and God weren't "officially involved," at least not according to the Constitution, the American people—Lincoln included—were telling a much different story. America's second "Come to Jesus," though it was a spiritual renewal, a season of church growth, evangelism, and widespread Jesus-induced conniptions, had a subtext that reconnected Christian values with American values. And even though many of America's largest denominations split apart, the love affair between God and America did not. In fact, in many ways the Civil War deepened our God-inspired national identity, unifying the bond between the ideals of America—liberty, justice, and the pursuit of happiness—and the ideals of Jesus: faith, hope, patience, and sobriety. Again, nowhere is this *patriotic-evangelical* partnership better communicated than in the lyrics of "The Battle Hymn of the Republic":

He has sounded forth the trumpet that shall never call retreat;
He is sifting out the hearts of men before His judgment seat;
Oh, be swift, my soul, to answer Him! be jubilant, my feet;
Our God is marching on.

When singing those words, the underlying mantra for many Americans was no less than this: *Thy America come, thy democracy be done, in Massachusetts as it is in Texas.* Though divided, wounded, and suffering from war fatigue, America's God was indeed marching on.

CHAPTER SEVEN

GOD'S AMERICAN FUNDAMENTALS

A fundamentalist is an evangelical Christian who is pissed off about something."[1] I stole that definition from George Marsden, who stole it from Jerry Falwell, who likely stole it from somebody else. The modern use of "fundamentalist" was coined in the 1920s when evangelicals began raging against science, specifically evolution, and biblical scholarship. Evangelicals become angry about all kinds of things today. Some fundamentalists even get angry when somebody has the audacity to call them a fundamentalist.

For example, Pastor Mark Driscoll hates when people call him that. In 2010, the pastor of Seattle's Mars Hill Church vociferated loudly his disgust for the movie *Avatar*. While James Cameron's propaganda-laced otherworldly adventure wasn't the greatest of all movie experiences, Driscoll called the film "the most demonic, satanic film" he'd ever seen. "That any Christian could watch that without seeing the overt demonism is beyond me." In recent years, Driscoll is best known for his YouTube videos, sermon clips of him ranting against yoga or screaming, "God hates you" at his congregation or confessing his ability to "see things"—*spiritual things*—horribly violent and mostly sexual *spiritual* things. Driscoll explains his *seeing things* as being "a whole other realm. It's like *The Matrix*.... You go into this whole other world.... I've seen women raped, I've seen children molested."[2]

Honestly, the visions that God gives Driscoll seem far more "demonic" than anything I witnessed in *Avatar*. Perhaps most telling about Driscoll's movie review was after he finished channeling his inner Falwell, when he followed his strong opinions with this: "Some of you [are thinking], 'This is my first time, is he a fundamentalist?'...I've been accused of many things, but not being a fundamentalist." While Falwell wore the label of "fundamentalist" like a badge of honor, Driscoll hates it, denying it even applies. How come? Why doesn't he, like so many fundamentalists of years gone by, own the designation with pride?

Driscoll both answered that question and put himself in the fundamentalist box during a 2007 interview with *Christianity Today*. "Fundamentalism is really losing the war," Driscoll said. Then, after blaming religious fundamentalism for popularizing liberal Christianity, he added, "A lot of what is fueling the left end of the emerging church is fatigue with hardcore fundamentalism that throws rocks at culture. But culture is the house that people live in, and it just seems really mean to keep throwing rocks at somebody's house."[3] So yes, Driscoll is a fundamentalist, even by his own definition.

Some Americans—most often, angry evangelicals—try to drain the word "fundamentalist" of its meaning. They attach it to non-Christian groups or individuals. They call Muslims fundamentalists. They call gay columnists or outspoken feminists fundamentalists. They avoid their own fundamentalist behavior by placing the label on those they can't control. And that's what fundamentalism is most often about: control. Fundamentalists use faith to dictate the behavior of others. They use their beliefs to legislate another person's life, story, or marital status. When a fundamentalist isn't in control, they don't know how to act. They become anxious and fearful when their country elects a president they didn't vote for. They turn angry and unreasonable when their churches open the doors to people with whom they disagree. Their survival is built upon a narcissistic perception that they are right and everybody who disagrees with them is wrong. The fundamentalist will almost always come into a situation knowing exactly what's right, what's good, what's holy, what's true, and, more importantly, what is and what isn't of God.

That's how the word "fundamentalism" got its start in the early twentieth century, when a group of evangelicals decided they needed to tell America what's what. According to Mark Noll, "The phrase [fundamentalism] came into prominence first when a widely circulated set of booklets called *The Fundamentals: A Testimony to the Truth* were published between 1910 and 1915."[4] Not surprisingly, God had a lot to say—more than a hundred articles, in fact, from a wide selection of white American evangelicals:

Together [the articles] defended the "fundamentals," or basics, of the faith that newer forms of thought had recently called into question, among them assertions that the Bible is the inspired Word of God; that Jesus Christ was God in human flesh, was born of a virgin, lived a sinless life, died on the cross for the salvation of men and women, rose from the dead, ascended into heaven, and would return at the end of the age in great glory; that sin is real and not the product of fevered imaginations; that God's grace and not human effort is the source of salvation; and that the church is God's institution designed to build up Christians and to spread the gospel.[5]

The authors of God's fundamentals were a who's who of theological conservatives, from B. B. Warfield to C. I. Scofield to R. A. Torrey. The men didn't agree on every detail about God, but they muted their differences "in order to publish *The Fundamentals*. Dispensationalists and confessional Calvinists, ecclesiastical separatists and loyal denominationalists, advocates of holiness and those wary of holiness themes all cooperated in this venture as a conserving response to the day's theological challenges."[6]

The fundamentals of God, an easy list of beliefs and ideas meant to separate the true Christians from the impostors, is an ideology born in the years following the Civil War, an American era that brought growth, misfortune, challenges, and new ways in which to think about God.

. . .

After the Civil War, God marched out of a catastrophe and headfirst into a huge mess. America was in shambles. Though our God wore the shiny exterior of the "Gilded Age," beneath God's sparkly surface, he was trying to calm a postwar storm. Though the war's effects ran deeper and lasted longer in America's South, a dark cloud of despair hung over much of the country. Lincoln's assassination made things worse. In the decades that followed, as America tried to reconstruct, the truth about our country's sins began floating to the surface.

America's Gilded Age was a duplicitous season in American history. For starters, racism ran amok in the South. Members of the former Confederacy's white Christian population attempted to find new ways to manage a newly freed people. States like South Carolina and Mississippi took legislative actions against black Americans, fearing the possibility of black domination. Hate, fear, and anger also fueled the rise of white supremacy groups, militant societies like the Ku Klux Klan who took matters of "white justice" into their own hands. Remember, the South was convinced that God was on their side, to the degree that the Confederate constitution included the words "invoking the favor of Almighty God" in the first sentence. Some historians believe that, by inserting God into their constitution, the Confederate states were offering a somewhat passive-aggressive rebuke of the federal Constitution for excluding God. Rather than heal, racial tensions only grew, paralyzing the South's full potential for over a century. However, racism also swarmed in the North, even among former abolitionists. Many Americans—those same God-fearing Americans who believed wholeheartedly that God hated slavery—still didn't think that black people should be granted the same rights, or at least to the same degree, under America's laws. For many black Americans, especially those newly freed after the war, life in a post–Civil War America was a new kind of hell. The violence they faced from racist white Christians wasn't even the half of it. Jobs were scarce. Housing and basic needs like food and clothes were, for many, difficult to find. For the vast majority of black Americans, especially those who were born into a life of slavery, adjusting to a life of freedom proved most challenging.

Other sins plagued American society. Anxiety and depression were on the rise. Many Americans were falling prey to secret addictions to alcohol and other recreational narcotics. As these addictions rose, so did child abuse, domestic abuse, homelessness, and divorce rates. America's journey forward was also strained by its repressive treatment toward women. From prostitution and abuse, to rape and sexual assault, to the denial of equal rights, God's so-called City Upon a Hill was in many places an unsafe environment for women.

.   .   .

But America didn't have a sin problem, not according to Phoebe Palmer. A Methodist minister from New York City, Palmer became convinced that America's real problem was a holiness deficiency. Palmer knew this because she was more or less a psychic, a *spiritually sensitive* soul since childhood. At age eleven, on a flap of her Bible, she wrote:

> *This revelation—holy, just, and true—*
> *Though oft I read, it seems forever new;*
> *While light from heaven upon its pages rest,*
> *I feel its power, and with it I am blessed.*
> *Henceforth, I take thee as my future guide,*
> *Let naught from thee my youthful heart divide.*
> *And then, if late or early death be mine,*
> *All will be well, since I, O Lord, am Thine!*

Her precocious spirit likely caused Phoebe Palmer to possess an ungodly love for theology, which ultimately led her to become a preacher (though not officially ordained by a denomination), author, and influential early advocate for women serving as preachers, pastors, and ministers of the Gospel. There was much debate regarding Palmer's gender and the Gospel, a war of words that mostly happened via tracts, short, concisely written essays published as small pocket-sized pamphlets. Since the time of the Puritans, theological and political debate happened in cities and communities through short published works, one side distributing its point of view and then a countering side writing, publishing, and distributing its own perspectives. Sometimes the debates went on for years.

Palmer's critics wrote vile appraisals about her ministry. Most of them criticized her theology, her preaching in public settings, and the fact that she didn't possess an Adam's apple. Even her supporters seemed uncertain about whether God really used women in ministry, often adding disclaimers about Palmer being one of God's special female exceptions. For that matter, she wasn't the greatest public speaker. Biographer Charles Edward White described her as "hesitant in speech and almost destitute of emotion in all her addresses and exercises."[7]

However, what Palmer lacked in talent, she made up for with a coldhearted determination. God was everything to this woman, sometimes to a psychotic fault. When three of her children died as infants (she also had three surviving children), she believed it was God's will for them to die. It wasn't that the preacher didn't grieve; she just came to accept the fact that God had killed her babies because she loved them more than she should have and had turned them into idols. That's how seriously Palmer took God, or how seriously she believed God took her.

Despite her demented understandings about God, Phoebe Palmer became a trailblazer for Christian perfectionism. Holiness, as she called it, became her ministerial calling card, the focus on which she founded most of her ministry. As a self-described scholar of Wesleyan theology—an Arminian-flavored ecclesiastical developed by John Wesley—Palmer believed, like Wesley, that the grace of God happened in two stages. God's first stage was the classic grace, the one that saved people, the grace that converted Buddhists, sadists, rapists, and Calvinists into Methodists. Then, after God's first grace was finished with the conversion process, he would send a second grace—like a booster shot—that converted former-Buddhists-*now*-Methodists into perfect Methodists. As it turned out, God's second grace was far better at making Methodists into perfectionists than making them into perfect Methodists. Still, in 1835, Palmer, along with her sister, Sarah Langford, started spreading God's Good News and God's Second Good News at their Tuesday evening Bible studies, dubbed "Tuesday Meeting for the Promotion of Holiness."

. . .

In time, Phoebe Palmer's message about God's holiness began to move away from the teachings of Wesley's "second grace." Wesleyan Methodists believe that individuals don't receive God's first and second grace at the same time. God wasn't a magician after all; the miracle of God's second grace happened over time, a process that could not be sped up or manufactured or turned into a formula. But Palmer contended that as soon as a person was fully consecrated unto God, that person could initiate faith and lay claim to 100 percent sanctification (another word for "second grace"). Using verses from the Book of Exodus and the Gospel of Matthew, biblical references alluding to one of Palmer's favorite "truths," that "the altar sanctifieth the gift," her "insta-sanctification" became so popular that in 1867 the Holiness movement was made official and Palmer was deemed "founding mother" of the movement.[8] Eventually the Holiness movement spawned two influential Christian groups—the Church of the Nazarene and, later, American Pentecostalism.

At some point in the middle of her life, Palmer became convinced that she was perfect, a spiritual reality she believed was a miracle of the Holy Spirit. A year before her death in 1874, she wrote, "I have an ever abiding conviction that I have received the sentence of death in myself." Palmer is referring to spiritual death, not the physical kind. In her mind, God had killed her fleshly self—the parts of her being capable of sinning and doubting—and replaced it with the Spirit of God. She was so convinced that God's Spirit possessed her body, she concluded, "that I should not trust myself"—because she couldn't trust herself, *she* wasn't there—"[that] the idea that I can do anything myself, seems so extinct, that the enemy is not apt to tempt me." Moreover, "so fully" did God consume Palmer's being and put "his seal upon it" that she believed "even Satan does not seem to question that my call is divine."

For Palmer, perfection came with a side effect: burning tongues. "I felt [the Holy Spirit's] consuming, hallowing, energizing influences fall on me, empowering me for holy activities and burning utterances."[9]

At this point, America had been promoting personal intimacy with God for more than a hundred years. Folks like Jonathan Edwards, George Whitefield, Francis Asbury, and others had aided in turning America's Christian intentions away from God's "communal relationships"—how the Puritans related to God—and helped shape Americans' relationships with God into more individual ones. In the 1800s, the Methodists and Baptists deepened America's commitment to individual connections with God, making Jesus the new face of American Christianity. And on those foundations, Phoebe Palmer began building something entirely new. According to Palmer, not only could one have a relationship with God, but that relationship—with help from the Holy Spirit!—came with some pretty miraculous applications, the most erroneous being "human perfection."[10] Under Palmer's guidance, America's faith made an emotional turn, a turn that began putting humans—"by faith"—in control of their own spiritual lives, their own happiness, and their own mortal and eternal destinies.

. . .

America's destiny was beginning to shine more brightly by the 1880s—not because of God exactly, but rather due to industry, technology, banking, and enterprise. The top 1 percent of Americans were becoming filthy rich, a reality that offered America a different kind of "rebirth." Frank Lambert writes, "[The Gilded Age] was a time of dazzling brilliance, manifested by the glittering wealth of those industrial magnates who made fortunes from steel, oil, railroads, finance, and shipping. These captains of industry were heralded for their enterprise and ingenuity in exploiting the great opportunities offered by a free market that rewarded their entrepreneurial ventures."[11]

Out of the ashes of a once war-torn America rose a new crop of national heroes, a list of names featuring the likes of Rockefeller, Carnegie, Vanderbilt, McCormick, and Morgan. Rather than Bibles and rifles, these men flashed wads of cash, expensive suits, and lifestyles that, to the average American, seemed like fairy tales. To those who didn't work for them, they brought America the kind of hope that people could feel, see, experience, and, best of all, spend.

But the Gilded Age wasn't all unicorns and rainbows. According to Lambert, "[Its] golden surface masked a dark and miserable underside of social inequities, wrenching poverty, and political corruption."[12] The underbelly of America's economic success, with no governmental involvement whatsoever, wasn't pretty. America's richest businessmen engaged in capitalism like hungry lions among sheep, greedily pouncing on America's free market with little concern for who or what they destroyed in the process. In addition to their unethical business strategies, many of their plants and factories were little more than sweatshops where men worked sixty-hour weeks in horrendous conditions and were paid, on average, ten cents an hour.

Eventually, during America's dance with prosperity, people started talking about what role the government should play amid the economic boom. As the number of Americans who experienced economic gains increased, so did the number living in poverty. But fixing the problem proved difficult. At the time, Washington, D.C., was crippled with political corruption. Anytime Congress attempted to regulate the free market, Big Business leaped passionately into the legislative process with cash on top of the table and sexual favors underneath. Mark Twain questioned the incestuous relationships between dirty politicians and greedy millionaires when he asked, "What is the chief end of man?—to get rich. In what way?—dishonestly if we can; honestly if we must."

.   .   .

Nowhere were the ills of the Gilded Age felt more deeply than in Chicago. The city's financial health moved from industrial and railway highs to the lows of riots and strikes. In the years leading up to the twentieth century, the Windy City experienced boom and bust, sometimes at the same time.

God spent a lot of time in Chicago during the Gilded Age. God's presence essentially began hovering over the capital of America's Midwest in 1856, the same year a certain nineteen-year-old named Dwight Lyman Moody moved to Chicago from Boston.

What was so special about D. L. Moody? For starters, his story represented one of the great American tales, the kind where a troubled kid drops out of school, discovers a knack for selling shoes, finds God, becomes a highly successful salesman, and then trades his successes to become one of the most legendary evangelists of all time. Moody is, by most accounts, the father of fundamentalist Christianity, a simpleton who dared to pursue evangelicalism with capitalistic ideals, and to take the first steps toward trademarking America's God.

That wasn't Moody's plan, however, not in the beginning. When he was twenty-three he traded in his "worldly possessions" to work at the Salvation Army in the Chicago slums. Choosing to sleep on the floors of church basements, eat a poor man's meager diet, and entertain the city's children with tricks and silly stories, Moody thrived on the streets of Chicago. Soon he would realize that God had far bigger plans for him.

. . .

By 1871, a Bible study that D. L. Moody crafted was reaching a couple thousand people on a weekly basis. A few years later, he and his ministry partner, Ira Sankey—a singer—were invited by a group of wealthy British evangelicals to lead a revival in Great Britain. This two-year evangelistic campaign with Sankey ended up changing his life. The well-publicized revivals were well advertised and promoted, multitudes of people attended, and the British press fell in love with Moody and Sankey. The news of their fame and success traveled fast. When the pair returned to the United States, America's press—religious and secular—was also smitten. Chicago's newspapers practically laid down palm leaves. That media exposure paid off. Soon after, some of America's richest citizens were aching to fund Moody's American tour. And Moody was more than happy to let them.

What made Moody's evangelistic mission unique was that he ran it like a business. Theologian Richard Kyle says that Moody systematized urban evangelism. "He galvanized into religious action church people in cities of millions.... He organized his revivals like a corporate CEO, leaving little to chance. There were committees for everything—prayer, finances, Bible study, visitation, music, ushering, tickets, and an executive committee to supervise the committees."[13]

Mixing business with God in this manner was unheard of in the late nineteenth century. Some people criticized Moody's advertising techniques, calling the very idea of religious advertising undignified. Moody shot back at one critic, telling him it was "more undignified to preach to empty pews." God and capitalism were kind to Moody, a combination that turned him into an American evangelical sensation. In some cities he was so popular that bigger venues were built or remodeled in anticipation for what God and Moody would do in their metropolis. Over the course of the late 1870s, Moody took God to Philadelphia, New York City, and Boston. Thousands attended the meetings. Chicago loved Moody so much that the city built him his own eight-thousand-person "tabernacle." He would ultimately require a new tabernacle for any city where he preached.[14]

Since Moody rarely passed an offering plate, to make his demands economically feasible he solicited funds from America's deepest pockets. This was no trouble for him either. The circles he walked in were many steps up the economic ladder from those he had known and befriended during his days at the Salvation Army. According to evangelical researcher Thomas Askew, "the list of Moody's sponsors reads like a roster of tycoons"— from J. P. Morgan and Cornelius Vanderbilt to John Wanamaker and Cyrus McCormick, just to name a few. Why were so many of Moody's rich friends willing to give so "sacrificially" to a revivalist? They believed in Moody's message, of course. Or, as Richard Kyle writes in *Evangelicalism*, "The social and labor unrest due to crowded urban areas and terrible working conditions made the business community nervous. They hoped that Moody's simple message would improve the morals of the 'unchurched masses' in the cities."[15]

Transforming his Gospel into motivational talks that helped the businessmen funding his mission was simple. When Moody railed passionately against drunkenness, he was, as Garry Wills writes, promoting good job performance.[16] During the riots, Moody often preached against joining unions or participating in strikes. He even helped promote the ten-hour workday, the American average during the Gilded Age. How did Moody accomplish this? By using "holy living" as the jumping-off point into a sermonizing plea such as this one:

Get something to do. If it is for fifteen hours a day, all the better; for while you are at work Satan does not have so much chance to tempt you. If you cannot earn more than a dollar a week, earn that. That is better than nothing, and you can pray to God for more.[17]

Not only did Moody take money from the very men whose businesses were creating impoverished urban environments, but he shaped God's message into "gilded" rhetoric that worked to silence the rich men's critics and the men they employed. Who better to make a poor man shut up and work harder than God?

The God that Moody promoted was one who made sin the family man's biggest problem. Everything came back to sin, according to Moody. From economic struggle to substance abuse to trouble at work, all of it was due to a person's sin. Moody's remedy was simple: Make good choices. According to the evangelist, God didn't help those who wouldn't help themselves. Many of Moody's ideas about God were laced with humanism, human effort, positive thinking, and right choices, all disguised as "faith in Jesus."

One of Moody's greatest influences on American Christianity was his mass evangelism. The techniques he created to promote and administer God at his revivals became the same ones Billy Graham would use seventy years later. According to Gary Wills, Moody was the first to successfully commercialize God. "He had a permanent staff in the dozens," writes Wills. "He formed a local executive committee and finance committee to organize resources. Advertisements were taken out in the newspapers.... He recruited well-drilled teams of ushers, one hundred to two hundred of them, wearing identifying ribbons and carrying long 'wands' to conduct people with.... Even the *Unitarian Review*, which had criticized him for 'commercializing' religion, had to admit, 'The thorough organization and clear business sense in this movement are to be admired.'"[18]

D. L. Moody fed God capitalism, fattened him up with

enterprising infrastructure, and gorged him with crusade-and-convention methodology, most of which still gets used in some fashion today. Moody industrialized God, made God into a free market advocate, and created his own evangelical empire that would become a blueprint for how ministry and evangelism would be done in the twentieth century. According to George Marsden, "Moody was not a sensationalist evangelist like Charles Finney before him or Billy Sunday in the next generation. Rather, he looked like one of the businessmen of the era and captivated his audiences with a homey and sentimental style of storytelling."[19]

Unlike the big-name evangelists who followed in his footsteps, Moody did not preach hellfire and brimstone. In fact, his relationship to the screaming pulpit-abusers was, as Marsden wrote, "both large and complex":

It could even be argued that [Moody] was [fundamentalism's] principal progenitor. He believed in biblical infallibility and pre-millennialism. He did as much as anyone in America to promote the forms of Holiness teaching and the ethical emphases that were accepted by many Fundamentalists. His closest associates had virtually all the traits of later Fundamentalism, and many of them participated directly in organizing the Fundamentalist movement in the twentieth century. Yet Moody himself lacked the one trait that was essential to a "Fundamentalist"—he was unalterably opposed to controversy.[20]

In many ways, D. L. Moody was ahead of his time. While doctrinally he was a fundamentalist through and through—he believed in the divine authority and literal interpretation of scripture, he believed in premillennialism, he believed in hell as an actual place, and he adhered to his "three theological

Rs" (ruined by sin, redeemed by Christ, and regenerated by the Holy Spirit)—he often covered up his harsh beliefs with quaint narratives and a flowery vernacular. As much as Moody is remembered as the "great American evangelist"—and that he was!—he should also be remembered for his remarkable ability to spin the message of God in whichever way might best fit the causes of capitalism, enterprise, and economic hierarchy. Because it's the latter that would affect God's American story, ushering in a culture where God, the Gospel, and greed walked hand in hand.

. . .

Meanwhile, the entire time God was working on the D. L. in Chicago, he was also scheming in St. Louis. God wasn't scheming alone, of course. America's God never schemes alone; there's always a human involved somewhere in the details. This time, God was plotting an idea with James H. Brookes, the seminary-trained pastor of Walnut Avenue Presbyterian Church. According to Brookes, God began opening his eyes to a new truth one morning after family devotions. As he and his family opened their Bibles to begin reading where they had left off the morning before, Brookes sighed. "The Book of Revelation." At the time, Brookes hated the last book of the Bible. "Because I do not understand it," he later wrote. "The book is so full of strange beasts and mysterious symbols, it does me no good." So that morning, rather than reading Revelation, he chose another passage.

After family devotions, Brookes started thinking too much. "Why did you omit the last book God has given us?" he asked himself. So the young preacher did what people always do when overwhelmed with God-related guilt; he began asking himself rhetorical questions. Among the questions was this one: "Did

God make a mistake in putting that book into the canon of sacred Scripture?"[21]

Feeling "convicted and condemned," Brookes "opened the book and read it through at a single sitting." Over the next few months, he began obsessing about the Book of Revelation, reading, taking notes, theorizing, and comparing the texts he read in Revelation to texts from Daniel, Jeremiah, Ezekiel, and others. His soul began to burn unnaturally for the Book of Revelation. During this "Revelation" season, he discovered the beginnings of an idea that would forever change the course of God in America. The "truth" hit Brookes like a lightning bolt: *Jesus is coming again* and *then again* a second time.

In James Brookes's day, the belief that "Jesus was returning" was not new. Most of America's Christians believed and taught that Jesus would return to earth at some point in the future. Up until then, this return was viewed as a spiritual "revelation," one that encouraged believers to be watchful and ever ready for their savior's "glorious appearing." The return of Christ was commonly viewed as a hopeful experience, a part of the "Good News." But Brookes helped to change all of that.

"Having gathered up the marked passages and brought them together," the Presbyterian minister "reached three conclusions":

First, Jesus Christ is coming back to this world as truly, bodily, visibly, personally as when He was born in Bethlehem of Judea.

Second, things shall not always be as they are now, but "nation shall not lift up a sword against nation, neither shall they learn war any more"; "The wolf shall dwell with the lamb and the leopard shall lie down with the kid"; "The inhabitants shall not say, I am sick; the people that dwell therein shall be forgiven their iniquity"; "The earth shall be filled with the knowledge of the glory of the Lord, as the waters cover the sea."

Third, this glorious change shall not precede, but succeed that glorious coming.[22]

In other words, Brookes became convinced that Jesus was going to return to earth not once, but *twice*. Which might seem trivial; however, a twice-returning Jesus changed everything.

. . .

At some point in the middle of his grandiose Revelation, James Brookes became preoccupied with the eschatological teachings of John Nelson Darby, a Plymouth Brethren pastor and theologian from London who had developed a theology called Dispensationalism. Darby's teachings confirmed Brookes's theory about Jesus's Second Coming. Since the early 1830s, Darby had worked endlessly to perfect his theological concepts regarding Jesus, the End of the World, and Zionism.

While Darby's doctrine had gained denominational footing across the pond in Great Britain, Brookes became America's promoter (considered by many to be "the American father") of Dispensationalism. According to Ernest Reisinger—a theologian who, in addition to thinking Darby's "dispensational" theories were biblical-based insanity, founded *Founders Journal*— Brookes and Darby met in person when Darby visited the United States in 1864 and again in 1865.[23] After meeting Darby, Brookes became America's chief advocate for Darby's premillennial message, which included the development of "a network of conferences and publications."[24]

Without question, John Nelson Darby is one of the most influential people in American history, quite an accomplishment considering he was British and spent only a limited amount of time in the United States. The founder of Dispensationalism is, like most influencers, touted among Americans as both saint and heretic. While Darby's teachings never fully caught on among Great Britain's believers, in America they flourished.

What made Darby's Dispensations so influential to American evangelicalism? For starters, Darby theologized the "Rapture." In fact, the Brit might have been the one who invented the idea. Either way, before Darby, nobody had ever heard of the "Rapture," let alone believed in it. Which is shocking, since more than 55 percent of Americans believe wholeheartedly in the Rapture today,[25] and more than 40 percent are convinced it will occur in our lifetime.[26]

Much speculation exists about where Darby's Rapture idea originated. While some historians credit his imagination, others suspect he borrowed/stole it. The uncertainty stems from the fact that two other accounts of the "Rapture theory" exist. Edward Irving, a minister of the Church of Scotland, began expounding on a Rapturesque concept in 1831, which was the same year that Darby began theorizing Jesus's two-appearance plan. Ironically, the third account—a more mystical conception of the "Rapture"—originated in Scotland too. Many believe that Irving may have received his manifestation from Margaret Macdonald, a fifteen-year-old Scottish prophetess who in 1830 received a vision of the "Rapture" as a message from God. Even though some believe Macdonald's "message from God" was actually a message from demons, her firsthand account sounds strikingly similar to the ideas that both Darby and Irving started dreaming up a year later. But according to Macdonald's account, which was first published in 1840's *Memoirs of James & George Macdonald of Port-Glasgow*, what the young woman "saw" included the following:

Suddenly what it was burst upon me with a glorious light
I saw it was just the Lord himself descending from Heaven
with a shout, just the glorified man....Many passages were
revealed, in a light in which I had not before seen them. I
repeated, "Now is the kingdom of Heaven like unto ten vir-
gins, who went forth to meet the Bridegroom...this is the
light to be kept burning—the light of God—that we may
discern that which cometh not with observation to the natural eye." Only those who have the light of God within
them will see the sign of his appearance... 'tis only those
that are alive in him that will be caught up to meet him
in the air. I saw that we must be in the Spirit, that we
might see spiritual things. John was in the Spirit, when he
saw a throne set in Heaven.—But I saw that the glory of
the ministration of the Spirit had not been known. I repeated frequently, but the spiritual temple must and shall be
reared, and the fullness of Christ be poured into his body,
and then shall we be caught up to meet him.[27]

Whether Macdonald's vision came from God, demons, or
too much scotch whiskey, what she saw described John Nelson
Darby's "Rapture" perfectly. Still, Darby is usually the one cred-
ited for making the Rapture famous and constructing an entire
eschatology around the concept, a lengthy expounding that included scripture references, graphs, and a potential timetable.

Darby believed that Jesus's first earthly appearance would be
a complete surprise, *like a thief in the night*. The point of Jesus's initial return would be to "rescue Church people" from the
apocalyptic events that would follow. According to him, God's
epic timetable is divided into seven separate dispensations, non-
uniform "ages" defined by how God interacts with humanity for
a specified number of years. The first dispensation began when
God created Adam and Eve, and lasted until the two were tossed

out of the Garden of Eden. Only God knows how long the first era—the dispensation of innocence—lasted, because only God knows how long Adam and Eve were well behaved. The second dispensation began the moment Adam and Even were kicked out of the Garden and lasted until the dispensation of government during Noah's time. Each dispensation varies in length, each according to a biblical timeline that Darby constructed. Today, according to Darby, we exist in the sixth era, which is the dispensation of grace. Darby taught that the era of grace began at the time of Jesus's crucifixion and will continue until the moment Jesus bursts through a sheet of stratocumulus clouds to the sound of trumpet, *like a thief in the night.*

According to John Nelson Darby, God, in addition to dispensations of time and a Rapture, is also putting together one hell of a grand finale, the Cirque du Soleil of divine judgment. Darby's God is basically a divine bully, a deity who was picked on as a kid and grew up to be a fat, egotistical king of kings who now sits on his throne chomping on turkey legs while torturing earth with his toes.

Barbara Rossing, a professor of New Testament at Lutheran School of Theology in Chicago, believes that Darby became convinced that God's "whole biblical plan for the end-times is already mapped out in the Old Testament." Rossing has spent a good portion of her academic career trying to debunk Darby's dispensational theories. In her book *The Rapture Exposed*, she writes, "The entire end-times framework of Darby's dispensationalist system is based on just three verses at the end of chapter 9 of Daniel!"[28] According to Rossing, the three verses from Daniel describe 490 years of Israel's history like this:

25 Know therefore and understand, that from the going forth of the commandment to restore and to build Jerusalem unto the Messiah the Prince shall be seven weeks,

and threescore and two weeks: the street shall be built again, and the wall, even in troublous times.

26 And after threescore and two weeks shall Messiah be cut off, but not for himself: and the people of the prince that shall come shall destroy the city and the sanctuary; and the end thereof shall be with a flood, and unto the end of the war desolations are determined.

27 And he shall confirm the covenant with many for one week: and in the midst of the week he shall cause the sacrifice and the oblation to cease, and for the overspreading of abominations he shall make it desolate, even until the consummation, and that determined shall be poured upon the desolate.

Even though most scholars of history and religion believe these verses describe a calamity that happened long ago—Rossing believes this happened when the tyrannical emperor Antiochus Epiphanes desecrated the Jewish temple and set up a statue of the Greek god Zeus in 168 B.C.,[29] Darby took the "chronology of seventy 'weeks' of Israel's history—with a day representing a year in this apocalyptic book" and turned it into God's diabolical future plan.[30] According to Darbyists, the seventieth week that Daniel refers to, the week when the Jewish temple is desecrated, has not happened yet. That event, according to Rossing's understanding of Darby's ideas, "remains 'unfulfilled prophecy,'" and is "awaiting fulfillment in some not-too-distant future time." Darby believed that 483 years of the Daniel prophecy were fulfilled in ancient Israel's history only up through week number sixty-nine.[31] *Da-da-da-DUHM*. Who or what messed up the final week in Daniel's "plan"? Jesus. Jesus threw a redemptive wrench into God's and Daniel's plans. But Jesus only pushed the pause button. Rossing explains Darby's "Messianic interruption" like this:

God paused the prophetic stopwatch for two thousand years because the Jews, who should have crowned Jesus as their Messiah and king, rejected him. God was forced to stop the clock and turn to a different plan, starting yet another dispensation of human history. With language like "God was forced," dispensationalists put God in a corner in a way that traditional theology would never permit—but a sense of prophetic inevitability is necessary for their system.[32]

The "dispensation of grace"—the age in which we are living now—is Jesus's pause. But Jesus is getting tired of pushing the pause button. Soon and very soon, God will tell him to push play, and that will be God's code for "Go rescue my people, son!" And as soon as the church has disappeared from Earth, those final seven years that Daniel wrote about thousands of years ago will resume as scheduled. Of course, those seven years will be the Great Tribulation, a seven-year God-induced horror show.

. . .

Dispensationalism became popular in America partly because of James Brookes, who promoted Darby's theories through seven books, 250 pamphlets, and his own periodical that he humbly called *The Truth*. Brookes also started a Bible conference in 1875, at which he indoctrinated young preachers with dispensational teachings.

But Brookes's greatest contribution to Darby's ideas happened when he personally introduced the biblical theories to a man named Cyrus I. Scofield. Scofield *loved* Darby's seventy-week, dispensationalized, Rapture-ready version of God. In fact, he loved Darby's God so much that he published in 1888 a booklet called *The Rightly Divided Word of God*, which basically explained in plain English what he believed God had written in Hebrew and Greek. Later, Scofield published his own King James Version "study Bible," which was God's Word with footnotes, added facts, biblical cross-referencing, and subheadings. All of Scofield's biblical extras—the headings, timelines, notes, explanations, and commentary—came from his dispensational worldview. First published in 1909, the Scofield Reference Bible has sold millions of copies worldwide and helped, along with William E. Blackstone's book *Jesus Is Coming*, to introduce America to a whole new way of thinking about God, America, and the Christian worldview.

Today, the Rapture and Dispensationalism are ingrained in America's social culture, a constant feeding frenzy of information, new "insights," and half-cocked ideas that keep a large portion of our country under the spell of prophecy, apocalypse, and current events. In the twentieth century, America's God has turned Dispensationalism into a multibillion-dollar spiritual obsession, a theology that evolved into a broad social ideal that eventually bled its way into nearly every aspect of the American lifestyle. From politics, science, and education to foreign affairs, tourism, and media, Dispensationalism affects the social core of American culture. It has taken American individualism to a whole new level, the subtext of God's message in this country turned from "it's all about God" to *it's all about us*. Because the ground zero of the dispensational belief system is that God is all about us. The Rapture is all about us. Jesus pushing the pause button is all about us. Even God's endgame, when he allegedly will unleash his justice of mass destruction on Planet Earth, is all about *us*—our vengeance on the society who wouldn't join us, vote like us, think like us, or even respect us.

With books like *Earth's Final Moments, Four Blood Moons, From Daniel to Doomsday, Can America Survive?,* and *Final*

Dawn over Jerusalem, San Antonio pastor John Hagee—one of today's dispensational kings—inspires his large following to become anxious and obsessed about topics such as the Middle East, America and Israel, and the End of the World. He's not alone, of course. There exists today an entire American subculture dedicated to the preoccupation of End Times prophecy, which includes books, movies, TV shows, DVD series, conferences, online communities, prophecy classes, and lots of sensational uses of the words "apocalypse," "battle," "judgment," and "wrath."

Few ideas have affected American society more deeply than John Nelson Darby's theories regarding the Rapture, Dispensationalism, and the End of Time. Darby's ideas not only changed how America's Christians thought about God and the Bible but also how they thought about the world. According to Scofield, Christians shouldn't worry about "the reformation of society." He said, "What Christ did not do, the Apostles did not do. Not one of them was a reformer."[33] Which is why so many of America's Christians do little to improve American society, because why bother when Jesus is coming back?

One reason the dispensational theory is so successful is that it can easily be integrated with or applied to current events. Darby's ideas about the Book of Revelation are in many ways allegorical in nature, an eschatological system that seems to apply perfectly to whatever era one lives in. Maybe that's because the Book of Revelation, according to many scholars and theologians, is actually meant to be an allegory, a story not about a literal event but one filled with mystery and promise and "truth" for any age. Maybe that's why the dispensational view of the End can be so easily applied to any point in history in the last hundred years. It's religious understanding that seems to transcend time and be easily applied to whatever headline is making news on any given day. In the 1930s and 1940s, America's dispensational prophets believed the Nazis were bringing the End. In the 1960s–1980s they foretold that the communists were bringing the End. And today all of the same Bible verses suggest that the Nations of Islam are bringing about the End. The only thing that has always been true about the prophecies of Dispensationalism is that they always create fear, anxiety, panic, converts, and some sort of "action plan" that keeps followers engaged.

God survived America's Gilded Age, but not without an expansive makeover. Toward the end of the twentieth century, Christianity in America would become defined by the doctrines of John Nelson Darby. Timothy Weber said, "Without millenarianism, there could not possibly be a Billy Graham, Oral Roberts, PTL Club, Jerry Falwell and Moral Majority, or any of a myriad of similar personages and movements."[34] That's largely true; Billy Graham became hooked on Darby's ideas, believing that "the whole world is hurtling toward a war greater than anything known before."[35] That was 1984. So far, that war hasn't come.

CHAPTER EIGHT

GOD'S MISSION ACCORDING TO AMERICA

In the early years of the twentieth century, God in America faced important questions, questions that many Americans are still asking today: Which is more important, feeding hungry people or evangelizing hungry people? In other words, is America's God concerned only with the souls of individuals, or does he also care about a person's basic needs like food, clean water, shelter, and a Wii? And if God does care about those latter things, are salvation and social reform compatible? And if so, how are they fashioned to work together? Because as George Marsden noted, "It was one thing to believe that Christians should organize for a better society; it was another to know exactly what would make a society better."[1]

In the early years of the twentieth century, urban missionaries were some of the first Christians to witness America's growing poverty in the guts of our country's cities. Many of the evangelists felt guilty about showing up at the homes of poor children with just the message of God. For one thing, the little ones couldn't eat God's Word, and furthermore, it was hard for them to concentrate on loving Jesus when their little tummies were growling.

Thirty or forty years earlier, D. L. Moody had phrased it this way:

> When I was at work for the City Relief Society...I used to go to a poor sinner with the Bible in one hand and a loaf of bread in the other....My idea was that I could open a poor man's heart by giving him a load of wood or a ton of coal when winter was coming on, but I soon found out that he wasn't any more interested in the Gospel on that account. Instead of thinking how he could come to Christ, he was thinking how long it would be before he got the load of wood. If I had the Bible in one hand and a loaf in the other, the people always looked first at the loaf, and that was just the contrary of the order laid down in the Gospel.[2]

At the time, Americans were accustomed to God being passive-aggressive and manipulative. Remember, D. L. Moody's philosophy was that a person's sin prevented God from providing them basic necessities. So to Moody and the large Christian entourage that followed him, winning a person to Jesus was better than feeding them or clothing them, because it was remedying the *real* problem, their sin. At times, Moody doesn't seem to fully grasp the meaning of his words or is so focused on the result that he's unable to comprehend how counterproductive and culturally damaging his tactics were. While it's hard to call his message the prosperity gospel, his version of the Christian faith was no doubt a forerunner to what would become significant messages for preachers like Jim Bakker and Benny Hinn. The Christianity that Moody taught worked like an economy. In God's economy, rather than supply and demand, the curves configured on the Kingdom of God's graphs portray connections between individuals' choices and their ability to *trust* God.

Today, a majority of America's evangelicals promote some

sort of free market version of faith, a culture of God that promotes a self-helping faith, a spiritualized humanism that puts "faith" in the hands and hearts of the individual. The core teaching of today's evangelicalism is a Jesus who is useless without *you*. *You* create your own destiny. *You* choose God. *You* make good choices or *you* make bad choices. *You* choose to believe in A, B, or C. But if you create an evangelical process—which works like Progressive Insurance: *you* put together your process by choosing from a selection of ideas that may or may not include books, small groups, counseling, intramural sports, community involvement, volunteerism, singing, theological discussions, and/or prayer—and *you* engage *your* process well, *you* will begin seeing good results, results some will call miraculous. These "miracles" will materialize in *your* life, family, job, financial situation, health, relationship, and, most of all, in *you*. But results vary, which might reflect *your* plan, *your* engagement of *your* plan, *your* choices, or *your* faith. Evangelicals are quick to give Jesus the glory when *your* plan succeeds, but it's never Jesus's fault when *your* plan fails. Because Jesus never fails. *You* do.

Somehow, a large population of America's evangelicals have become convinced that this process is the ideal Christian life.

· · ·

Not all of America's Christians felt the same way. Some believed that Christians had a responsibility to help poor people live sustainable lives. And many of the radical thinkers who preached America's Social Gospel weren't opposed to asking the U.S. government to help the good cause, either. As George Marsden explains, the Social Gospel "explicitly rejected the individualism and laissez-faire economics that had prevailed in the Gilded Age and insisted rather that the government take an active part in alleviating the harshest effects of an unrestrained free enterprise system."[3]

Like many of God's American ideas, the Social Gospel movement originated in Great Britain. One of its earliest proponents was Frederick Denison Maurice, a Christian socialist and theologian, who believed that when Jesus prayed, "Thy Kingdom come, thy will be done, *on earth* as it is in Heaven," he meant it. In his book *Kingdom of God*, he advocated on behalf of impoverished people, suggesting that a Christian's responsibility on earth was to bless the poor, the meek, and so forth.[4] Maurice's passions became the taglines for God's "Social Gospel" in America. Episcopalians and Congregationalists were the first to jump on board. America's Catholics were active in socializing God too.

However, one of America's most vocal Social Gospel advocates was a Baptist named Walter Rauschenbusch, who authored the Social Gospel's handbook, *Christianity and the Social Crisis*, in 1907:

> It is wholly in harmony with any true conception of the life of Jesus to believe that his conception of the kingdom became vaster and truer as he worked for the kingdom.... [Jesus] remained a social hope. The kingdom of God is still a collective conception involving the whole social life of man. It is not a matter of saving human atoms, but of saving the social organism. It is not a matter of getting individuals to heaven, but of transforming the life on earth into the harmony of Heaven.[5]

The harmony of heaven that Rauschenbusch outlined would not be an easy sell, considering his Social Jesus was being crucified over and over again by louder and more popular evangelicals. For instance, Russell H. Conwell, also a Baptist—one who pastored the largest Protestant church in America—preached a popular sermon called "Acres of Diamonds." Conwell believed that "to make money honestly is to preach the Gospel." Not only did Conwell's God promote economic growth, but he offered a return on investment:

> Money is power, and you ought to be reasonably ambitious to have it....Money printed your Bible, money builds your churches, money sends your missionaries, and money pays your preachers....I am always willing that my church should raise my salary, because the church that pays the largest salary always raises it the easiest....The man who gets the largest salary can do the most good with the power that is furnished to him....If you can honestly attain unto riches...it is your Christian and godly duty to do so....Some men say, "Don't you sympathize with the poor?" Of course I do...but the number of poor who are to be sympathized with is very small. To sympathize with a man whom God has punished for his sins, thus to help him when God would still continue a just punishment, is to do wrong, no doubt about it, and we do that more than we help those who are deserving. While we should sympathize with God's poor—that is, those who cannot help themselves—let us remember there is not a poor person in the United States who was not made poor by his own shortcomings, or by the shortcomings of someone else. It is all wrong to be poor, anyhow.[6]

Conwell's ideas about being poor were popular Christian thinking in the early twentieth century, which is why the Social Gospel was considered controversial among Christians living in a culture where "get rich" was fast becoming America's new morality. Yet another division was beginning to form, one that jutted America's Ultra-Evangelical God against America's new Semi-Progressive God.

. . .

In 1912, Billy Sunday, America's favorite evangelical preacher at the time, delivered one of his hellfire-and-brimstone revivals in Columbus, Ohio. In the years before World War I, Sunday was America's most popular voice for God, a divine prophetic celebrity who scared people into loving God. Sunday summed up his beliefs in a sermon called "Old Time Religion," comparing his own reverence to some of the most famous names of Christian history:

> I believe the Bible is the word of God from cover to cover. I believe that the man who magnifies the Word of God in his preaching is the man whom God will honor. Why do. such names stand out on the pages of history as Wesley, Whitefield, Finney and Martin Luther? Because of their fearless denunciation of all sin, and because they preach Jesus Christ without fear or favor.[7]

Despite the American people favoring Billy Sunday's scrappy sermonizing, not everybody was impressed. Members of the religious elite called his messages trite, devoid of theological substance, lacking in compassion, and little more than "flippant evangelism."[8] A former financial supporter of Sunday's, Dr. Hugh Morrison, called his onetime friend's preaching "a crass theology, an un-Christian temper...extreme sensationalism and a blood-curdling irreverence."[9] Even Helen Keller thought Sunday was vile, calling him "a monkey wrench [thrown] in the social revolution."[10] Criticism didn't affect Sunday much, at least not publicly. When a Unitarian pastor described Sunday as "wretchedly vulgar," Sunday mocked him in front of seventy-five thousand people. "Vulgar, eh?" he retorted. "We shall see. Let the fussy preachers rave.... Bah for the critics. They'll get theirs."[11] That was his way of saying, *Go to hell!*

After Billy Sunday's Columbus revival, one well-loved local pastor offered his criticism in a letter to the editor of the *National Bulletin*. In that letter, Pastor Washington Gladden rallied against Sunday's tactics, suggesting they were malicious and that the evangelist's fans were brainwashed. "Mr. Sunday [could] send men to Hell by platoons, right and left, day after day, and these good brethren [would] listen and applaud."[12] The *Bulletin* averred that Gladden was "a man of the highest intellectual gifts and of great personal force and independence of character."[13] The pastor of Columbus's First Congregational Church was an early supporter of the Social Gospel movement, well known for standing up for the American worker and challenging the business practices of wealthy people long before it was popular. In *Working People and Their Employers*, Gladden wrote that it was the Christian minister's responsibility "to protest, in the name of Jesus of Nazareth, against the division of the Church and society into jealous and unsympathizing classes."[14] When Sunday read Gladden's review, he went on the defense, suggesting they were "trying to make a religion out of social service with Jesus Christ left out."

At the time, America's God couldn't decide who he was—a social reformer or an evangelizer. In 2011, Dr. Ron Sider, a Canadian-born theologian who teaches holistic ministry and public policy at Palmer Theological Seminary in Pennsylvania[15]—told *Relevant* magazine that he believes the line between doing good and sharing the Gospel is nonexistent. According to Sider, God prefers a more holistic approach to ministry. "People are both spiritual and material beings," said Sider, and "addressing only half of the problem only gives you half of the solution." Sider thinks that God expects Americans to sacrifice freely, that doing so would vastly change the world we live in. "We know how to reduce poverty—it's just a matter of resources."[16]

In the early twentieth century, God and America didn't know how to reduce poverty. God's and America's resources were limited too. Walter Rauschenbusch—that progressive Baptist—thought it was America's economic and social sins that were standing in the way of holy progress. He believed America's "principalities and powers" were greedy and only interested in helping themselves. He believed the only solution for the country was to come under the "law of Christ."[17] According to Rauschenbusch, this law not only included humility, compassion, peace, love, and one day Christian rock and roll, but also socialism. Rauschenbusch's Jesus was far too Marxist for America's faithful, or as Stephen Prothero puts it, "[He] was a progressive activist going into battle against the collective sins of a capitalist society. His hero lorded over not only the home and the church but also the shop and the factory."[18]

. . .

America's evangelicals were too busy with their own causes to take seriously Rauschenbusch's social views about Jesus. Most evangelicals believed that America's primary problem was not poverty, but disobedience. Chief among the country's sins were drinking beer and not keeping the sabbath holy. To that end, God started raging against America's lust for alcoholic beverages. And of course, God won—well, for thirteen years, he won. Evangelicals considered Prohibition the greatest American achievement since winning the War of Independence against Great Britain. Billy Sunday was ecstatic about Prohibition. In fact, according to the revivalist it was he who single-handedly defeated the enemies who manufactured, sold, and transported hell's poison in America. In Sunday's defense, he did preach often about how much God hated liquor. The subject of "booze" became Sunday's bread-and-butter topic, an impassioned plea that made him an influential voice in the Prohibition movement. However, some believe that Sunday's "Prohibition victory" backfired, as his success as America's evangelist began a swift decline after 1920. Though he no doubt helped the cause, the Prohibition Act passed largely because of the tireless, not always ethical political dealings of Wayne Wheeler, a liberal believer who organized the Anti-Saloon League.

The campaign to control and/or end America's consumption of alcohol grew more popular toward the end of the Gilded Age. This was due primarily to the influx of bars, saloons, taverns, and pubs in cities like Philadelphia, Baltimore, Chicago, Boston, and New York City. While evangelicals waged war because booze was Satan's venom, progressive Christians joined the fight because they were convinced that America's emerging drinking culture was creating urban environments fertile for prostitution, domestic abuse, and unnecessary street violence among hotheaded (and intoxicated) young people. Still, the two groups worked together. Their union was a cautious one, however, neither side fully trusting the intentions and methods of the other.

After years of legal battles between wet and dry states, drunk and sober legislators, and a much-divided American public, Congress passed the Eighteenth Amendment in 1919 and enacted into law the National Prohibition Act of 1920. And no doubt God smiled, though likely in moderation, because even though this battle for social reform brought countless religious folks together for one cause, it also brought into question the true motives of America's God. How much control over the lives of Americans did God truly desire? And to what lengths was God willing to go to mandate laws regarding Americans' behavior? America's Christians are still answering these questions, always looking for ways in which to sneak "faith" into the legislative process, hoping that by limiting the freedoms of others they can protect and constitute their own.

. . .

In the first chapter of the Book of Acts, Jesus is quoted as saying, "But ye shall receive power, after that the Holy Ghost is come upon you: and ye shall be witnesses unto me both in Jerusalem, and in all Judaea, and in Samaria, and unto the uttermost part of the earth."[19] America's Christians love that verse. They take it very seriously. Leading up to the twentieth century, Americans began taking it too seriously, dreaming about what the nation's role could become. Some Christians became convinced that it was time for America to win the world for Jesus Christ.

America's evangelicals were giddy with excitement about the prospect of the "ends of the earth" becoming Christian. Against Indian tribes, America had long shown how cruel, violent, and evangelistic its imperialistic nature could be, but the general assumption was that the Pacific Ocean would be a natural stopping point. By the end of the nineteenth century, Americans began to imagine how our democratic Christianity might work in countries around the world. Though most denominations were already supporting missionaries in every continent except Antarctica, the practice was for the most part seen as a Baptist mission or a Methodist mission or a Presbyterian mission. Of course, these missions didn't involve military force or a congressional vote, just proselytizing, preachers, and building churches. However, was it possible that God and America could somehow work together on a Christ-centered foreign affairs operation? The evangelicals were likely thinking, "Hell yeah!" Believe it or not, most progressive Christians loved the idea, too, thinking, *How could freedom and Jesus be a bad thing?*

It's not clear who made the final decision, but at some point during the latter part of the Gilded Age, the Kingdom of God transformed from a domestic interest to a global one. Denominational missionary work was one thing, but the U.S. government spreading the Good American News of Jesus was quite another. Two of the earliest Social Gospel supporters of Christ-centered imperialism were Josiah Strong and Lyman Abbott, both ministers in the Congregational Church.

In 1885, Josiah Strong published *Our Country: Its Possible Future and Its Present Crisis*, a fear-filled thesis loaded with racist overtones and God-conquering ideas. But those discrepancies didn't keep *Our Country* from turning into one of the most influential Social Gospel books of the age. The way he saw it, diversity was America's greatest enemy. While others touted America's growth, Strong believed that increased immigration would do little more than muddy America's strong moral character, our devout ties to God, our patriotic sensibilities, and worst of all, the gene pool. Strong wrote that the United States was "destined to dispossess many weaker races, assimilate others, and mold the remainder until, in a very true and important sense, it has Anglo-Saxonized mankind."[20] In order to keep this dream alive, he concluded that the only remedy was to "Christianize the immigrant," believing *that* would help the new resident "be easily Americanized."[21] Strong's greatest fears involved America's cities. "Our cities," he said, "which are gathering together the most dangerous elements of our civilization, will, in due time, unless Christianized, prove the destruction of our free institutions."[22] Strong viewed evangelizing not simply as a spiritual concern; to him it was a national endeavor. The only way to ensure peaceful, homogeneous thinking and to protect America's people would be to guard them from foreign DNA. Strong believed that Jesus was "God's final and complete solution to the dark problem of heathenism among many inferior people."[23]

Like Strong, Lyman Abbott also used his talent for writing to engrave his political spirituality upon the culture. Pastor Abbott just so happened to be the editor of *The Outlook*, the most influential American periodical focusing on politics and religion. Though Abbott's words weren't nearly as Hitleresque as Strong's, he often wrote about America's destiny using Darwinian terminology, describing our nation as one that was *evolving* to new heights of spirituality and greater understanding of *reason*. It was his perspective that Americans would be doing the world a disservice if they didn't douse it with democratic evangelicalism. When President William McKinley decided that a bloody war was a small price to pay for securing ownership of the Philippines, Abbott cheered, calling it a "noble" step "in the development of the human brotherhood."[24]

Upon winning control of the Philippines, our twenty-fifth U.S. president paced the White House floors for nights, wondering what he was going to do with an Asian archipelago. "I am not ashamed to tell you, gentlemen," McKinley wrote, "that I went down on my knees and prayed [to] Almighty God for light and guidance more than one night. And one night late [the answer] came to me this way—I don't know how it was, but it came."

What did God tell President McKinley to do with the Philippines? God's answer came in four parts. First, God told McKinley that he was not to give the islands back to Spain, for that "would be cowardly and dishonorable." Second, God didn't want France or Germany getting them either, because they were America's "commercial rivals in the Orient," which "would be bad business and discreditable." Third, God told McKinley that America "could not leave [the Philippines] to themselves." Why? Because "they were unfit for self-government." Last, God told McKinley "there was nothing left for [America] to do but to take them all and to educate the Filipinos and uplift and civilize and Christianize them, and by God's grace do the very best we could by them, as our fellow men for whom Christ also died."[25] And what, pray tell, was God's best for the Philippines? Bloody calamity, that's what. Historian Stuart Creighton Miller called the conquest "Armageddon, 1900."[26] Mark Twain mourned that "we have debauched America's honor and blackened her face before the world."[27]

McKinley was assassinated long before he had the chance to fully realize how awful his perfect will of God would be. Was our evangelical travesty in Southeast Asia really the perfect will of God for America? For the Philippines? More importantly, who in their right minds would fall in love with a Jesus who arrives with guns and waging a war strategy? The answers to those questions depend on whom you ask.

. . .

Despite having blood on our hands, America's Christians— liberal and conservative alike—would continue to promote God and Country, putting patriotism right next to godly and holy living. In most Christian circles, those who questioned America's international evangelical missions were considered heretics.

Eighteen years later, when America entered World War I, every one of its religious denominations except Mennonites and Quakers (they were pacifists) supported the decision to go to war. Billy Sunday skipped around for days after he heard of America's decision. In fact, Sunday practically became the war's unofficial spokesperson, declaring multiple times that "Christianity and patriotism are synonymous terms" and "hell and traitors are synonymous" too.[28] He even used the war to make punch lines, laughing at himself whenever he said, "If you turn Hell upside down, you will find *Made in Germany* stamped on the bottom."[29] Billy Sunday's greatest travesty was that he dumbed God down to silly and thoughtless antics. God and Jesus were just a part of a schtick that he used to talk about any topic, from hell to war, from liquor to morality. But as Mark Noll points out, the fundamentalists weren't the only Christian patriots loading Jesus into the guns of soldiers. Noll writes, "No less direct was a doyen of American religious liberalism, Shailer Mathews of the University of Chicago Divinity School." According to Mathews, "for an American to refuse to share in the present war ... [he] is not Christian."[30]

Congregational minister William Barton turned the Great War into a battle between the world's ideas and Jesus. After quoting from books by Treitschke, Nietzsche, Bernhardi, and Clausewitz, Barton laid the titles on his pulpit and claimed that "the great question now to be settled in this present war is whether the future is to be dominated by the ideals of these four books, or this other one, the Holy Bible, the Gospel of Jesus Christ."[31] By the time he finished preaching, he'd taken his congregation to the front lines of the battle, handed them pistols, and declared with the intensity of Mel Gibson in *Braveheart* that this was why America was fighting:

We are fighting for nothing less than the inherent rights of mankind. We are fighting to rebuke the affirmation that treaties are to be regarded as scraps of paper. We are fighting to disprove the alleged right of large nations to gain their place in the sun at the expense of small nations' place on the map. We are fighting for the freedom of the seas. We are fighting for the sanctity of the soil. We are fighting that the world may rise above the wicked and cruel despotism that now crushes it, from the load of armament and wasteful taxation that now overburdens it, to the enjoyment of an abiding peace that is based upon righteousness and international justice. We have a righteous cause, an unselfish cause, a cause worth sacrifice and devotion. We are fighting for the heritage of humanity.[32]

In 1918, Lyman Abbott published *The Twentieth Century Crusade*, a 110-page justification for the Great War. "The question," said Abbott, "is war right or wrong, is like the question, was the crucifixion the greatest crime or the greatest glory of human history." In other words, rhetorical. According to Abbott and God, the war was a crusade, and the crusade was a fight that people were constantly engaging in, whether on the battlefield or in their own home or in the depths of the soul—"we are all born on a field of battle." Abbott, over eighty years old when he wrote *Crusade*, had seen a lot of history happen on his journey. In that book we get a clearer perspective as to why he believed war played an important role in America's Social Gospel:

During my lifetime...slavery has been abolished...the public school system has been extended into every State and territory of our country, and so developed as to afford equal benefits for both sexes and all classes and all vocations. The public lands have been thrown open to settlers by our homestead law.... Child labor has been forbidden, the right of workers to organize for the protection of their rights and the promotion of their interest has been recognized by law...and suffrage has been so extended that it is either absolutely free or subject to such qualifications as can easily be met by a reasonable degree of industry and thrift.... He who believes that God is in his world, that above all earthly plans and purposes there is One who gives to his children their ideals and inspires them with their courage, and that history is in very truth the working out of his plans for his children, will find despair for the world impossible.

He who looks back only four years may find in those four years food for his doubts and discouragements, but he who looks back a hundred years must have a great genius for pessimism if he can doubt in what direction the unseen forces are carrying the human race.[33]

Eventually, Abbott did answer the question: Does God approve of our war? The answer was a resounding "Yes!" Of course the war was justified by God. In fact, Abbott believed that "a crusade to make this world a home in which God's children can live in peace and safety is more Christian than a crusade to recover from pagans the tomb in which the body of Christ was buried."[34] And with that, Abbott justified practically every war from then until Kingdom Come.

Politicians didn't have to sell World War I to America. America's churches sold the war to America. Whether our cause was just or not was never the issue. The church practically jumped at the chance to promote America's wars as *holy wars*, offering theological context, scriptural text, and God's consent to a large and captive audience. Some Christian leaders even turned the soldier into America's new missionary. One Baptist pastor in California said, "I look upon the enlistment of an American soldier as I do on the departure of a missionary to Burma."[35] Any countering view was considered treasonous and therefore silenced.

It is ironic, considering how many of them love war today, that staunch Dispensationalists were the last Christian group to become pro-war. Their initial stand was, as Methodist Arno Clemens Gaebelein contended, that "the world was too far gone and that true believers should avoid meddling in 'man's plans during man's day.'"[36] But Dispensationalists couldn't handle being called anti-American for long. Soon their antiwar stance crumbled under the pressure and they too joined the "Christian" cause. George Marsden believed this was an important development, as "the premillennialists played such a central role in organizing fundamentalism immediately after the war, that a close look at their wartime views was most helpful for understanding the relationship between fundamentalism and its cultural context." In other words, the war helped to unite the nation's premillennial fundamentalists with its postmillennial fundamentalists, and they eventually became a mighty and influential throng known simply as America's fundamentalists.[37]

. . .

When God and America returned home from fighting World War I, the years that followed would bring a very different war, a kind of American conflict that would eventually fuel Bill O'Reilly's career as a conservative commentator on Fox News. It's hard to say when exactly America's Christians began fighting culture wars, but America's official love interest in protecting God and his property legislatively hit a boiling point in 1925. Riding a postwar high, America's fundamentalist evangelicals turned their sights toward Darwin's theory of evolution. As a majority of America's Christians saw it, there was no greater enemy to their beliefs than those who sought to undermine Christianity's most important doctrine—the inerrancy of God's Word, the A.V. 1611 King James Bible. For evangelical fundamentalists, to suggest that even one word of the Bible did not exit the mouth of God was the same as throwing the whole book into the garbage can. To the fundamentalist Christian, the Bible is God and God is the Bible.

God's plan to protect his Word from America's sins was to pursue passing a law that made it illegal to teach Darwin's theory of evolution in public schools. The man God chose to complete the deed was William Jennings Bryan, a career politician from Nebraska. Bryan was a Democrat who had not only served as a member of Congress and as the secretary of state under Woodrow Wilson but had unsuccessfully run for president of the United States three times. Bryan joining ranks with America's fundamentalists didn't make sense, really. This was a man who championed a long list of causes—women's suffrage, a federal income tax, the League of Nations, and opposition to capital punishment—that most fundamentalists rallied passionately against. Garry Wills says that Bryan embraced the legislative fight against Darwin's evolution because "he thought of it as a relativistic and 'Nietzschean' assault on morals, without knowing much about either science or the Bible."[38] Nonetheless, fundamentalists welcomed Bryan's decision to rage against evolution. Even Billy Sunday wrote him a personal "thank-you." Though Bryan was a talented politician successful at rallying support from both sides of the aisle, his ignorance regarding the complexities of this debate proved too much for his political brilliance.

Ultimately, Bryan's brilliance was tested in the Scopes Trial—known in the beginning as *The State of Tennessee v. John Thomas Scopes*. The case was mostly a publicity stunt, one that worked far better than anybody anticipated. It started when Tennessee teacher John T. Scopes, on behalf of the American Civil Liberties Union (ACLU), volunteered to violate the Butler Act, legislation that made it illegal to teach evolution in state-sponsored schools. At the time, the ACLU was right smack in the middle of a campaign to stop public school textbooks from being purged of Darwinism. With Scopes, they were just hoping to spark a civil lawsuit, something that might put them in the position to challenge the constitutionality of the ban. But then Scopes decided that he didn't mind getting arrested, which turned the whole thing into a criminal case. Meanwhile, after learning about the trial in Tennessee, Clarence Darrow, a lawyer from Illinois, along with his friend H. L. Mencken, a journalist for the *Baltimore Sun*, decided to jump in bed with the ACLU. Darrow brought his legal forces down to Tennessee to defend Scopes, and Mencken brought his journalist friends to ensure that the nation would hear every single detail of the case. This was exactly what the ACLU was hoping would happen. The trial was broadcast on national radio. And the scenes outside the courtroom soon turned into a circus.

Then Darrow put Bryan on the stand as an "expert witness" in support of the Bible's inerrancy. He used the Bible against the great politician, exposing Bryan's ignorance about the truthfulness and accuracy of the biblical stories. Yet in the end the jury ended up convicting Scopes of the charges against him. This was exactly what the ACLU expected, and they planned to appeal the case to the Supreme Court. But Bryan's biblical testimony was so damning that the Tennessee Supreme Court voided the conviction on a technicality. A few days after the verdict was announced, Bryan died in his sleep.

For fundamentalists, the Scopes Trial was a huge blow to their political and spiritual egos. Nobody expected their hatred for Darwin and evolution to turn into a live-broadcasted three-ring circus act against God Almighty, a trial that God lost on a technicality. From the public's perspective, God lost fair and square. Bryan's poor performance as a witness on behalf of God's Word knocked fundamentalism down a few pegs. But the defeat didn't kill it entirely.

· · ·

In the decades following the Scopes Trial, as America became engulfed by the Great Depression and then the Second World War, Christians once again became unified under the cause of warfare. The Gospel of "bring down the Axis" was as Christian as singing "Jesus Loves Me." Unlike the last war, this war needed no theologizing. Japan's strike against Pearl Harbor trumped America's need for God's approval. Religious unity beset much of America's culture. "God bless our troops" became the banner that Christians waved proudly.

In the 1940s, amid our national unanimity, God's attention was on domestic concerns as well. Among evangelical thinkers, God took interest in teenagers, helping to launch a national campaign called Youth for Christ (YFC). This effort helped to launch the evangelical career of Billy Graham, as he was YFC's first full-time employee. God also helped to further socialize America's Catholics during this time. While the prejudices between the nation's Protestants and America's Catholics have never fully vanished, the 1940s and 1950s found America's bigger population warming up to their transubstantiation-believing brothers and sisters. After World War II, John Tracy Ellis, a priest, writer, and influential advocate against anti-Catholic sentiment in America, helped to ignite an intellectual movement among America's Catholics, urging them to make education one of their core agendas. The number of Americans converting to Catholicism soared in the decade after the war, influenced in part by Thomas Merton's *The Seven Storey Mountain*, the best-selling book about Merton's conversion and life as a monk.

. . .

The spiritually focused philosophies of Reinhold Niebuhr flourished during this lull, especially among America's more enlightened congregations. There, the religious insights of Niebuhr—a Missouri-born pastor, social reformer, professor, and cultural critic—inundated the more elite circles of America's high-minded Christians. Theologically, he fell somewhere between liberals and conservatives, fusing beliefs about God, morality, and the human condition. Niebuhr supported America's quest for justice against the Nazi regime in Europe, but in 1946, on behalf of the Federal Council of Churches, he outlined and signed an official statement regarding the United States' decision to drop atomic bombs on Hiroshima and Nagasaki, an action he believed was "morally indefensible."[39]

Some of Niebuhr's writings became a part of the very fabric of American Christianity, most notably this prayer: *God, grant me the serenity to accept the things I cannot change, the courage to change the things I can, and the wisdom to know the difference.* (I, too, was a bit surprised to learn that those words didn't appear in the Book of Psalms.) But while the majority of Niebuhr's concepts were not suitable fodder for Hallmark cards and Home Interiors plaques, his spiritual wisdom did indeed seep ever so emphatically into the spiritual conversations of American history. Challenging theologies and doctrines on both sides of the spiritual aisle—"Comfort the afflicted, and afflict the comfortable" was one of his mottos—Niebuhr's ideas blend Jesus and Christian truth with a compassionate common sense. Regarding Niebuhr's concepts about Jesus, Mark Noll writes, "In the person of Christ, Niebuhr found a unique example of an individual who used power only for good and not—as all other people—for evil. The cross of Christ was a particularly important theme for Niebuhr since it reveals the great paradox of powerlessness turned into power."[40] Niebuhr saved his harshest critique for America's religious right, warning harshly against America's "dreams of managing history" as well as our misplaced "Messianic consciousness" in how we handle our foreign affairs. In the years following World War II, Niebuhr believed that America continued to exist as "an adolescent nation, with illusions of innocency." That, for him, was *The Irony of American History*, the title of his 1952 book, one of his most celebrated works. And while much of the book offered insight and opinion about America's foreign policies, Niebuhr's true effect on America's God might be the way he effortlessly blended psychology and spirituality:

> Nothing that is worth doing can be achieved in our lifetime; therefore we must be saved by hope. Nothing which is true or beautiful or good makes complete sense in any immediate context of history; therefore we must be saved by faith. Nothing we do, however virtuous, can be accomplished alone; therefore we must be saved by love. No virtuous act is quite as virtuous from the standpoint of our friend or foe as it is from our standpoint. Therefore we must be saved by the final form of love which is forgiveness.[41]

Niebuhr theologized a progressive worldview but did so while offering a very present concept of "sin" or "evil." That was his chief frustration with religious liberals in America—they placed so much trust in human wisdom and virtue that they crippled their ability to deal with evil.[42] Frank Lambert puts it this way: "Niebuhr pointed out that events such as the Great Depression, two world wars, and the Cold War made a mockery of the liberal faith in progress. He and other Christian realists reminded men and women that sin had hardly been stamped out, and the transcendent God was the world's only sure hope against destruction."[43]

The theologies of Niebuhr are still influential today. Not only was Jimmy Carter a fan, but in 2007, then senator Barack Obama was asked by *New York Times* columnist David Brooks if he'd ever read anything by Niebuhr. Obama's response? "He's one of my favorite philosophers." Brooks then asked, "What do you take away from him?" The man who would a year later become the leader of the free world said, "I take away the compelling idea that there's serious evil in the world, and hardship and pain. And we should be humble and modest in our belief we can eliminate those things. But we shouldn't use that as an excuse for cynicism and inaction. I take away...the sense we have to make these efforts knowing they are hard, and not swinging from naïve idealism to bitter realism."[44]

In an America that was getting ready to enter a spiritual season in which the reign of religious thinkers would become defined by the ideals of folks like Billy Graham, Oral Roberts, John R. Rice, Bob Jones Sr., Jerry Falwell, Pat Robertson, and Rick Warren, Niebuhr's words are like a prophetic challenge:

> Politics always aims at some kind of harmony or balance of interest, and such a harmony cannot be regarded as directly related to the final harmony of love of the Kingdom of God. All men are naturally inclined to obscure the morally ambiguous element in their political cause by investing it with religious sanctity. This is why religion is more frequently a source of confusion than of light in the political realm. The tendency to equate our political with our Christian convictions causes politics to generate idolatry.[45]

What Reinhold Niebuhr described became a key component of the future of God in America: that Christians would one day sync Christianity with politics. And while from Niebuhr's perspective this narrative of God—one that holily connected faith with politics, Jesus with national moralism—was already a well-established American ideal, in the decades following his death (in 1971), the nationalized conservative Jesus he "foretold" would become the idol that Americans would ask into their hearts.

The narrative of America's God was growing, but it was growing out of control, evolving into a philosophy and faith that could easily become shaped by whomever and into whatever the culture demanded.

CHAPTER NINE

HOLY AMERICAN SPIRIT!

According to the man sitting at the table next to me at Starbucks, the Holy Spirit was planning a trip to Chicago. "Two weeks from today, it's going to get crazy up in here," the man said with a straight face. The woman he was talking to kept nodding, seeming to agree with every word. When he said, "We're gonna take back Chi-town for God," the woman swooned like Eastern Europeans sitting in the front row at a Michael Jackson concert. "I've been praying nonstop for this event," she said. "Last night I was praying so hard that I woke up my roommate. It was over-the-top intense."

Eventually, after spending twenty minutes gushing and giggling about how excited they were to be organizing their church's outdoor worship event, the two coordinators started talking details. I'm not certain, but from the sound of it, these two had booked the Holy Spirit before. Not only did they know exactly what an appearance of the Holy Spirit required, but they seemed quite prepared and eager to micromanage God's Spirit for three and a half hours. They began working through a lengthy checklist of things they needed for the event, a list that, among a host of other things, included three thousand boxes of Kleenex, fifteen hundred bottles of water, twenty-five hundred

New Testament Bibles, three stationary paramedic tents and two mobile paramedic units, stage security (professional and volunteers), a K-9 drug unit, and eight stretch limos. I took notes. The longer I listened, the more the Holy Spirit sounded like a diva.

But that wasn't the first time I'd thought such a thing. Considering the Holy Spirit is the member of the Godhead whom people of faith use most often when attempting to Christianize things like holy wars and patriotism, capitalism and get-rich-quick schemes, magical powers and The End of the World, it's easy to see why the Spirit of God might be high-maintenance, demanding, and difficult to contain.

Later, before the couple's meeting was finished, they grabbed each other's hands and prayed. For seven minutes they prayed. I counted. And they prayed a mouthful. By the time they finished praying, Chicago's crime, poverty, and unemployment rates had disappeared; every gay, lesbian, bisexual, transgendered, and queer person living within a sixty-mile radius had been "healed" of their sexuality; the Holy Spirit had zoomed through the hallways of every Chicago hospital and healed people with cancers, tumors, skin disorders; STDs, autoimmune deficiencies, autism, and bipolar disorder; and, "most importantly," God's Spirit had put on such a marvelous display of "grace so lavish" and "power so mind-numbing" that all of Chicago, every sinner and saint, had become entranced by the realization that they needed to surrender their lives to God. And then they said amen.

• • •

In 1906, according to a group of charismatic believers, God started inhabiting an old abandoned Methodist church located at 312 Azusa Street in the industrial district of Los Angeles. There, under the spiritual leadership of William J. Seymour—a black holiness preacher—another new movement of God was beginning to catch fire. Seymour's church, the Apostolic Faith Gospel Mission, was quickly becoming the talk of the town. Something was different about God when he visited California. He was happier, less focused on theology and doctrine, and quite passionate about people experiencing baptisms of "the Holy Ghost and fire."[1] Dunking people in the scorching-hot presence of the Holy Ghost wasn't new. In fact, the Holiness movement had been performing the new sacrament for years in places like Topeka and Dallas. According to Seymour, Christians needed to receive the Baptism of the Holy Ghost in order to become holy, sanctified, more like Jesus, and, by some people's standards, worthy of being admitted to the local insane asylum. Before moving to L.A., Seymour had learned how to wield God's Flaming Spirit under the direction of Charles Fox Parham, whose ministry was a hybrid of Methodist and Holiness influences. Parham influenced God because, according to him, God's special sign that an individual had been baptized in God's Hot Spirit was the heaven-certified gift of tongues, a spiritual language that people uttered that only the Holy Spirit could understand and translate. Under the tutelage of Parham (in Kansas) and Seymour (in California), God also began issuing spiritual gifts to people: gifts of healing, gifts of discernment, gifts of miracles, and gifts of prophecy.

Before Seymour's movement became a church and a spiritual crusade that would one day affect hundreds of millions of people worldwide, God's presence in California began as a small Bible study. On April 9, 1906, Seymour and a small group of African American believers gathered together in a house for prayer and preaching in downtown L.A. Seymour preached on the gift of tongues, a sermon inspired by the Book of Acts, chapter two, verse four: "And they were all filled with the Holy Ghost, and began to speak with other tongues, as the Spirit gave them utterance." After the talk, Seymour and the others sat in the living room of the house and waited for God's Ghost to show up. And eventually he did. The first thing God did was inhabit the body of a man named Edward C. Lee. Filled up with the Spirit of God, Lee began mumbling nonsensical words that nobody except God could comprehend. Moments later, Jennie Evans Moore, a woman sitting two people over from Lee, became possessed by the Holy Ghost too. Moore described the experience this way: "It seemed as if a vessel broke within me and water surged up through my being which, when it reached my mouth came out in a torrent of speech in languages God had given me."[2] According to Moore's diary entry, God's Spirit gushed out of her mouth like water out of a fire hydrant. God gifted her with multilingual abilities, deluging the room with messages in French, Spanish, Latin, Greek, Hebrew, and Hindustani. And God's Spirit didn't stop there. It pushed Moore up out of her seat, scooted her across the room, and sat her down in front of a piano. "I played and sang under inspiration," she wrote, "although I had not learned to play."

God's appearance in that house created a commotion, one that began seeping into other parts of the city. The opinions about the Holy Ghost's appearance were mixed. Some folks were convinced that the Day of Pentecost was beginning to fall on Los Angeles. Others thought the "signs" were heresy, demons loosed by Satan to woo Christians into a web of lies. Still, more people showed up the following week. A year later, more than fifteen hundred people—black and white, young and old—were showing up for services at Seymour's church.

As the movement grew, uniting people in the Holy Spirit, it also created division. Families broke apart. Sons and daughters became estranged from mothers and fathers. But the news of what was happening on Azusa Street continued to spread. God began showing up in Holy Ghost manifestations in both the black and white communities of Los Angeles. "One of its most prominent features," writes Mark Noll, "was the full participation of women in public activities." And "in an America that still took racial barriers for granted, Azusa Street was also remarkable for the striking way in which blacks and whites joined to participate in its nightly meetings."[3]

. . .

Surprisingly, one of the Azusa Revival's biggest critics ended up being Pastor Parham, the very man who'd inspired Pastor Seymour's Pentecostalism. In October 1906, Parham traveled to L.A. to experience the revival for himself. Despite being the pastor who inspired the mighty "God buzz" intoxicating hundreds of people in Topeka, the Holy Spirit crazy happening in L.A.—the euphoric praying and out-of-control dancing—appalled him. However, he was most outraged by the sight of black Americans worshiping hand in hand with white Americans. Parham, a Ku Klux Klan ally, labeled the spectacle "Southern darky camp meetings." After that, Seymour and Parham no longer worked together.

While Parham's critique left little effect on the Azusa church, his words did foreshadow a future hostility amid the Pentecostal Church. Many of the Pentecostal churches that formed in those early years were made up of racially diverse congregations, but that quickly changed. Soon America's Pentecostal God began following America's cultural trend toward segregation, eventually dividing into two major denominations, the Assemblies of God for white people and the Church of God in Christ for black.

Though the "racial lines" among some Pentecostal denominations still exist, America's Pentecostals have in many ways put to shame every other religious movement in America when it comes to racial diversity. While the Pentecostal record on race relations is stained, with a long list of grave and costly mistakes, that doesn't negate the fact that many of America's most diverse and multicultural churches and denominations are indeed charismatic congregations. While America's church as a whole has a long way to go in desegregating its churches, denominations, and culture, Pentecostals are much farther down that road than most.

Frank Bartleman was one of the white people whom Parham witnessed worshiping at Azusa. Having moved to California in 1904, Bartleman had become disillusioned by the divisions he witnessed in America's churches. As one who believed that "the color line has been washed away in the Blood,"[4] he seemed particularly concerned with racial division:

> Every fresh division or party in the church gives to the world a contradiction as to the oneness of the body of Christ, and the truthfulness of the Gospel. Multitudes are bowing down and burning incense to a doctrine rather than Christ.... The Spirit is laboring for the unity of believers today, for the "one body," that the prayer of Jesus may be answered, "that they all may be one, that the world may believe."[5]

After reading about and becoming enamored with the rumors of revival happening across the Atlantic in Wales, Bartleman once again started to search for spiritual awakening. Hoping and praying that whatever was happening in Wales would one day become reality in Los Angeles, he was eventually led by his curiosity to Seymour's church. Though he was a trained minister, Bartleman's true passion was writing. His words detail with honesty the successes and struggles that the Holy Ghost experienced in Los Angeles:

> There was a general spirit of humility manifested in the meeting. They were taken up with God. Evidently the

Lord had found the little company at last, outside as always, through whom He could have His way. God had not chosen an established mission where this could be done. They were in the hands of men; the Spirit could not work. Others far more pretentious had failed. That which man esteems had been passed by once more, and the Spirit was born again in a humble "stable," outside ecclesiastical establishments.[6]

As Bartleman tells the story, God's Holy Ghost power started running out of fuel in late 1907. Upon returning from the preaching circuit, he came back to L.A. and discovered that "the work [at Azusa] had fallen back considerably." The church was in awful shape. Not only were "the saints...badly split up...[but] the Spirit was [also] bound."[7] Bartleman was saddened by what he saw, but he wasn't surprised. He had long feared that beneath the emotionally colorful and unconventional display, God's California dream was in trouble. *Big* trouble. The environment he had once praised as humble and covered in prayer—a kind of place where "Satan cannot live"—had evolved into something ugly and not made by God. Bartleman noticed a dramatic shift beginning to take shape at Azusa. "As the movement began to wane," he wrote, "platforms were built higher, coattails were worn longer, choirs were organized, and string bands came into existence to 'jazz' the people."[8] Later, he explained Azusa's demise like this:

Man always adds to the message God has given. This is Satan's chief way to discredit and destroy it....Men are creatures of extremes. The message generally suffers more from its friends than from its foes. We have this treasure in "earthen vessels." The truth can always be abused.[9]

Most of Azusa's members believed that the chief abuser of truth was Brother Seymour. So while their pastor vacationed out east, a new pastor stepped in. William H. Durham from Chicago came to town and started running services. The Spirit of God was back! Until Brother Seymour returned. As Bartleman wrote, "I went to Azusa Street and to everyone's surprise found the doors all locked, with chain and padlock. Brother Seymour had hastened back from the east and, with his trustees, decided to lock Brother Durham out. It was his message they objected to. But they locked God and the saints out from the old cradle of power also."[10] As soon as Brother Durham found another building, a thousand people joined him at the new location. However, by 1911 the people had turned on Brother Durham, which eventually led to his stepping down. But not without having his say—or, as he believed, God's say:

A great crisis is now on. Men do not see the plan of God in the present Pentecostal movement. Such a complete revolution is necessary that it staggers them. They are unwilling to see that which they have labored so hard to build up thrown down; but before God's plans can be carried out, man's plans must be set aside.... The great question is, will men see the plan of God and yield to it?... Let God's people everywhere begin to seek in deep, true humility.... The people who really humble themselves, and stand the test, God will use to do His work.[11]

Whether it was God's work or the work of humble Pentecostals passing the test of time is difficult to say. But whatever it was, it was spreading across America. Embracing the words of the Prophet Joel—"I will pour out my spirit upon all flesh"—the Pentecostal movement exploded onto America's religious scene, bringing new spirited life to old religious ideas and putting human emotion at the forefront of America's Christianity. Azusa Street wasn't the first time Americans dabbled in Holy Spirit theatrics like dancing and speaking in tongues. God's Spirit was the behind the spectacle that befell Cane Ridge, Kentucky, and no doubt the member of the Trinity who spearheaded Phoebe Palmer's Holiness pursuit that came later. In the eighteenth century, Mother Ann Lee's Shakers—a group of believers who followed Lee from England to New York—frequently spoke in a spiritual language others couldn't understand. The Holiness movement—later called Pentecostalism—built its traditions and ideas upon Wesley's legacy of Christian perfection, a teaching that proclaimed that faultless sanctification could happen to anybody who was justified (or "saved"). Influenced by the Keswick movement in England, America's Holy People began preaching about a "third blessing," an act of grace they called "Baptism in the Holy Spirit," which became evident in a person's life when they spoke in tongues.[12] While the spiritual gift of tongues is as old as Christianity itself—Harold Bloom suspects "even older"[13]—the revival on Azusa Street popularized the gift of unknown tongues and revolutionized the spiritual habit into a homegrown American prototype, a spiritual idea that could easily become franchised in locations across America (and eventually the world).

· · ·

But what was the Holy Spirit planning to do with America's Pentecostals? Heck, what was the Holy Spirit planning to do with America's God? At the time nobody knew, nor did they seem to care. As long as the bodies of Americans were being ransacked by the Holy Ghost, that was all that mattered. For many Pentecostals, anything less than "keep on keeping on" was considered weakness, sin even. America's first Pentecostals rarely looked back on the mistakes they had made yesterday. Instead, they focused on what worked, and with that, they lived by the Spirit moment by moment and moved forward.

Unlike most of America's religious movements, twentieth-century Pentecostalism was not founded on theology and doctrine. That's not to say that it did not have a theology. In truth, within the body of the Assemblies of God denomination (the largest and most influential Pentecostal Church), the Pentecostal theology evolved early. Douglas Sweeney explains the transition this way:

> One of the most important features of AG's early history was the approval of William Durham's understanding of sanctification.... Most early Pentecostals held to a Wesleyan view of sanctification as the fruit of a momentous second blessing. But Durham argued for what he preferred to call "the finished work of Calvary." Repudiating the need for a second work of special grace (i.e., subsequent to conversion)—or even the goal of instantaneous consecration unto the Lord—Durham claimed that Christ's atoning work ("the finished work of Calvary") is available at conversion and appropriated over the course of an "overcoming life."[14]

But Sweeney also acknowledged that theology and/or doctrine had never been the binding element of the Pentecostal Church. "Over the past one hundred years...most Pentecostals have deemphasized the doctrine of sanctification, stressing instead their common witness to the baptism in the Spirit and the higher Christian life that it empowers."[15] In the end, the Pentecostal pastors who spread out toward various corners of the country were not selling a "thinking spirituality." The Gospel they promoted was much more of a "feeling spirituality," which was why

Pentecostalism offered ministers of various kinds a pathway toward fame, fortune, and celebrity status, because their cause, though rooted in fundamentalist viewpoints, was to help people "experience" God's Spirit. Since many of the earliest Pentecostal pastors lacked education, the Spirit came with few limits and fewer instructions.

This makes sense. Believing that it was impossible for humans to control God's Spirit seems far more "all powerful" than a Holy Spirit that could be manipulated and downgraded by a list of rules, requirements, and human prejudices. Being unconfined by limits and instructions gave Pentecostalism a freer environment for gender and racial equality.

Without boundaries, the Holy Spirit flourished in America, and while some people scoffed at the Holy Spectacle, others rejoiced, danced, shouted, and became engulfed by the new spiritual wave.

. . .

But there was one problem: Sometimes the Holy Spirit made a mess and didn't clean up after itself. The mess that God's Spirit left behind on Azusa Street was just the beginning. Other messes would follow. One Sunday morning in 1910, a Pentecostal preacher from Tennessee named George W. Hensley, "Little George" for short, stood in front of his congregation and sermonized his passionate belief in the words of Jesus from the Gospel of Mark, chapter sixteen:

In my name shall they cast out devils; they shall speak with new tongues; they shall take up serpents; and if they drink any deadly thing, it shall not hurt them; they shall lay hands on the sick, and they shall recover.

Although Little George possessed very minimal reading and comprehension skills, what he could understand from the Bible, he understood as literal. A few weeks prior to preaching this sermon, he had visited an outdoor church service. There he witnessed a man handling a poisonous snake without being bitten. Bewildered, Little George questioned his own faith and was curious about whether he needed to risk his life in order to test the validity of his spiritual affections. A few days later God led him to climb to the top of White Oak Mountain in East Tennessee in search of a serpent. At a place called Rainbow Rock, he found one. Some people allege that upon seeing the rattlesnake, Little George knelt down a few feet from the snake and prayed to God, asking him to remove his fear by anointing him with "the power." Snake handlers today believe God answered Little George's prayer, that nothing could have harmed him that day. They say Little George—the godfather of snake handling—was protected by the armor of the Lord. Maybe he was, since he was able to grab the large reptile and hold it in "trembling hands" long enough to put it in a box and carry it down the mountain. Days later, after he was finished delivering a rousing declaration about how Jesus said that true believers should speak in tongues, exorcise demons, and perform miraculous healings, he pulled the rattlesnake out of the box with his bare hands. The congregation was spellbound and Little George was just getting started. After handling the snake for a few minutes, he commanded every member of his church to handle it also or be "doomed to eternal hell."[16]

Among Pentecostals living in Appalachia, Little George became a celebrity. He traveled all over preaching his sermons, encouraging a movement of people to trust Jesus enough to "take up serpents." And people did, even after the practice became illegal. When Little George was seventy-five, while he was preaching a sermon in Florida, the Holy Ghost moved on him to pick up the snake he kept in a lard can. For fifteen minutes he handled the large eastern diamondback rattlesnake, placing it atop his head, rubbing it against his face, and dangling it around his neck. As he was returning the snake to the can, it struck him on his wrist. Little George's arm swelled up and turned pitch black, and he began to vomit blood. He refused medical treatment. "I'll be saved by my faith," he said. "I won't go to the hospital for anything." The following morning, right before he died, Little George told his fourth wife, "I know I am going. It is God's will."[17] The latest preacher to die from a Holy Spirit–induced snakebite was Mack Wolford, a Pentecostal pastor from West Virginia who was struck by his pet snake at an outdoor worship service in 2012.

Today God-induced snake handling only happens at a handful of churches throughout Appalachia. Though it never caught on as much as Little George wanted, it didn't leave America's God unaffected. The snake handlers turned their version of God into a freak show, a display of faith that became little more than a fear- and risk-drenched circus act. And while the majority of Pentecostals still ran away from venomous reptiles, they didn't run from using the other Spirit-filled works that Jesus mentioned in Mark 16—the safer, more ambiguous options—to turn their church services into holy faith entertainment. Soon, the American Pentecostal experience was one built on big expectations, miraculous anticipation, and the "it" factors of those spearheading the Holy Ghost's power.

. . .

In 1923, God launched the evangelical career of Aimee Semple McPherson, the Holy Spirit–filled pastor of Long Beach, California's Angelus Temple. As the spiritual leader at Angelus, the onetime Canadian captivated California's faithful with her flamboyant displays of biblical proclamations, a popularity that eventually necessitated the erection of three more churches in the Los Angeles area. And by God, McPherson was just beginning! Not only did McPherson's ministry eventually launch the Foursquare Church, a charismatic denomination that today boasts more than seventeen hundred congregations, but she also became the first evangelical to utilize the power of media to advance God's Kingdom. As one of the first women to receive a broadcasting license from the FCC, McPherson took her Foursquare message, one that promoted the "four roles of Jesus: as Savior, Baptizer, Healer, and Coming King,"[18] to the radio airwaves. The Pentecostal darling became America's inspirational voice in the wilderness, rivaling the fame of nearly every famous evangelical—male or female—of her time. Even while America was drowning in the throes of the Great Depression, McPherson's Holy Ghost–financed empire allowed her the privilege of owning several houses and an extensive wardrobe usually reserved for the politically powerful or the Hollywood elite.

Theatrics became one of McPherson's spiritual trump cards. In 1934, she premiered her God-and-America show before a sold-out crowd at L.A.'s famed Shrine Auditorium. The performance was split into two parts. Part One retold McPherson's version of America's Christian history. Using drama, orchestral numbers, and extravagant props and costuming, the production included scenes that reenacted the Pilgrims landing at Plymouth Rock, America's Founding Fathers—George, Ben, and Thomas, all portrayed as Christians reading their Bibles—writing the Constitution, and a much-distressed Abraham Lincoln on his knees, praying desperately for God's patriotic guidance. McPherson was no historian, so some parts of her *America* were so riddled with conservative ideology and Christianized patriotism that her portrayal would have made Rick Santorum blush. But then Act One took a not-so-subtle turn. In order to keep the audience's attention, America's "Good News" needed tension—lots of it—so McPherson offered scene after scene showcasing our country's sin-wrecked breakdown. McPherson's *America* suffered a plethora of problems, from modernization, gambling, divorce rates, and drunkenness to evolution, Catholicism, atheism, and liberal theology. The way McPherson told the country's story, God and America were filing for divorce. Why? Because God's *O Beautiful* was having multiple "affairs," engaging in unholy liaisons with all of God's enemies. "[The enemy is] determined to blot out the God who had led and nurtured the United States," one of the actors declared.[19]

Then, as the orchestra paused dramatically and a hush fell over the crowd, a malicious character appeared on the stage, a man portraying both an atheist and a communist, and if that wasn't enough, the godless commie was carrying a hammer, a chisel, and a bucket of paint. *What was this terrorist going to do?*

[The man tiptoed] up to an oversized dollar bill and...chipped away the words "In God We Trust." Then he sneaked over to a massive poster featuring the lines of the national anthem. He reached down, grabbed a brush, and began splattering red paint across all references to God.[20]

Watching in horror, the audience booed at the sight of that no-good socialist defiling the documents and ideas that, according to the drama's narrator, were "the very blood and body of our nation—the very foundation upon which it has stood through the years."[21] Part One's final scene featured an enormous replica of the U.S. Capitol building—the enemy's *real* target. Atop the replica flew an American flag. The evildoer climbed atop the U.S. Capitol and removed the American flag, and, much to the dismay of the audience, he replaced our nation's flag with a *red* flag, symbolizing the country's descent into communism.[22]

But just as America's faith, hope, and future seemed lost, there came Act Two, which featured none other than the Almighty Aimee Semple McPherson. The crowd went wild. Once they calmed down, Sister Aimee smiled, bowed, and with the raspy exuberant passion of Oprah giving away new cars, she shouted, "America! Awake! The enemy is at your gates! They have penetrated your walls! America! You are in danger! An enemy power is penetrating your strongholds! There is death in their hands—the bombs of atheism and of communism and of anarchy! America! Awake! Defend your own!"[23]

That's when a man portraying Uncle Sam ran onto the stage, tackled the enemy, and announced that the little devil was being issued a one-way ticket back to Red Russia.

McPherson's drama was staged on November 2, 1934, just a few days prior to Californians going to the polls to elect a governor. Supporters of Frank Merriam, the Republican incumbent, had grown concerned that their man's Democratic rival, author Upton Sinclair, was gaining political ground. McPherson's program—a mix of politics, God, and "Hollywood pizzazz"—was the grand finale in a series of political attacks that California Republicans waged against Sinclair. Sister Aimee was more than happy to sacrifice her pastoral services for the good of the Republican Party. McPherson became one of the most influential conduits between God and Republican politics, a role she played throughout her ministry career.

· · ·

Aimee McPherson was the quintessential Pentecostal revivalist, a vibrant personality who possessed a natural sense of showmanship, miraculous healing power, and an exuberant sense of style, occasionally donning a long robelike dress complete with a cross embroidered across her chest like the Superman insignia. But sadly, as with so many of America's most charismatic evangelists, her spiritual significance was often overshadowed by controversy, stories that include a mystery-laden "kidnapping" in 1926[24] and rumors of numerous affairs, sometimes with big-name celebrities. Sister Aimee died in 1944 from an overdose of barbiturates. But despite her strange and gaudy approach to baptizing America in Holy Ghost fire and her tragic end, McPherson's influence on the future functionality of Pentecostalism was incomparable. She was a trailblazer, a preacher who not only helped to connect the dots between evangelism and conservative politics, but also championed the manner in which millions of people would fall in love with the Holy Spirit, through drama, style, pizzazz, and a mother lode of passion.

Milton Berle may have defined best McPherson's influence on God. In his autobiography, the comedian claimed to have met the preacher at a charity event at the Shrine Auditorium. According to Berle, they developed a short-lived friendship, one that Berle said resulted in two sexual encounters. After one of those encounters, Berle recalled that McPherson stuck out her hand and said, "Good luck with your show, Milton." Berle couldn't resist the setup. He responded, "Good luck with yours, Aimee."[25]

· · ·

After Aimee McPherson's death, the Holy Spirit's American career continued to evolve into a variety of different American spiritualisms. In 1947, God and Oral Roberts started peddling the country together, setting up tents, preaching the Gospel, and allegedly healing thousands of people. The dynamic Kathryn Kuhlman was also wowing audiences throughout the heartland with her unique blend of preaching, magic tricks, and psychic abilities. Kuhlman's core message? Complete surrender, a human action that the evangelist promised brought results. "I surrendered unto [God] all there was of me; everything!" she said, claiming that in that moment she "realized what it meant to have real power."

Pentecostals rarely encourage people to give up anything without promising something in return. Many Pentecostals preach some variation of what Kate Bowler says has many names, "from the slightly pejorative (Health and Wealth or Name It and Claim It) to the vaguely descriptive (Faith or Word of Faith) to the blunt shorthand, the prosperity gospel."[26] Bowler says that although it's difficult to define, it's easy to find. "The prosperity gospel is a wildly popular Christian message of spiritual, physical, and financial mastery that dominates not only much of the American religious scene but some of the largest churches around the globe."[27]

Few ideas have molded Americans' understanding about God more than the Gospel of Prosperity. That's not surprising. It's easy to see why spirituality with the promise of blessings of varying kinds would become a popular doctrine, especially among Americans. The roots of this so-called Gospel can be traced back to the turn of the twentieth century, to a minister named Essek William Kenyon, a revivalist and educator whose life mission was helping Christians unlock God's treasure chest of blessings. Like many of America's earliest Holy Spirit promoters, Kenyon was influenced by Phoebe Palmer's Holiness movement and Azusa's baptism of the Holy Spirit. But unlike many of his righteous peers, Kenyon was highly educated, a graduate of Emerson College of Oratory in Boston. There, it's believed that he came in contact with "New England sage Ralph Waldo Trine and other metaphysical teachers"[28] and was introduced to New Thought (also called Higher Thought), a philosophy that, in its most basic form, adheres to the idea that God is everywhere, in all of us, and is a faceless energy that manifests itself perfectly and equally within all creation. Years later, Kenyon would merge elements of New Thought theology with his own evangelical theology to create a Christianized version of "mind-power."[29] Based on this spiritual logic, Kenyon believed he opened up the floodgates of God's blessings: holy favors of health, wealth, and positive feelings. Positive thinking, or "overcoming faith," as Kenyon called it, caught on slowly, eventually picking up steam and popularity after World War II.

Even though Jesus talked about storing up treasures in heaven, many of America's preachers during the 1950s and 1960s were caught up in the emerging prosperity gospel movement. And it wasn't just the Pentecostals mixing spiritual voodoo with biblical Christianity, either. Episcopalians, Methodists, and Lutherans dabbled with the Holy Spirit too. The teachings that many of these evangelists promoted involved faith mixed with positive-thinking tactics, meditative practices, and mindfulness techniques. One popular Episcopalian speaker and author, Agnes Sanford, became well known for helping audiences align with God's light through mental and physical practices. Sanford said that "the first step in seeking to produce results by any power is to contact that power.... The second step is to turn it on.... The third step is to believe that this power is coming into use and to accept it by faith."[30]

Spiritual oneness with the divine was all well and good, and that certainly still sells in today's God Market, but for many believers, the good-thinking pursuit was too whimsical and lacked practicality. This is why preachers of the charismatic movements began directing their theological mindfulness toward money, success, and health and wellness. Folks like Jim and Tammy Faye Bakker, Paul and Jan Crouch, Oral Roberts, Ernest Angley, Benny Hinn, and Pat Robertson built up small television kingdoms based on what televangelist Kenneth Copeland declared was the good news for the poor: "Jesus has come and they don't have to be poor anymore!"[31] Oral Roberts put the good news like this: "God wants you well. God wants you prosperous. God wants you a whole person."

Today, the voices of God's prosperity include evangelists like Paula White, Rod Parsley, and Jesse Duplantis. Duplantis is quite a character. Not only does the Louisiana pastor swear on a stack of Bibles that Jesus once gave him a personal tour of heaven, but he also loves boasting about his own personal abundance. "I've never had the Lord say, 'Jesse, I think that car is a little bit too nice.' I've had vehicles and the Lord said, 'Would you please go park that at your house. Don't put that in front of my house. I don't want people to think that I'm a poor God.'"[32] But Duplantis isn't the only prosperity preacher who has uttered craziness in the name of God and money. Pastor Leroy Thompson loves money so much he told his congregation that "God said, 'It is time to tell the money you don't belong to the wicked, you belong to us.'...Money come to me now!"[33]

In 2013, the Oxygen network debuted *Preachers of L.A.*, a reality show that follows the lives of six successful Los Angeles pastors as they experience the prosperity gospel in all of its glory, abundance, fashion, and drama. One of the show's subjects is Bishop Clarence McClendon, who declares, "The Bible says I wish above all things that you would prosper and be in health, even as your soul prospers. I believe that." Cast member Bishop Ron Gibson agrees. The former gang member turned pastor says, "P. Diddy, Jay-Z, they're not the only ones who should be driving Ferraris and living in large houses."[34]

Perhaps this was what the Reverend John Cotton was prophesying in his sermon "God's Promise to His Plantation." Preaching to the future Boston colonists days before setting sail to the New World, Cotton told them that God was going to plant a mighty forest. Is Cotton's God the same God that Pastor Jay Haizlip promotes in Huntington Beach, California? According to the star of *Preachers of L.A.*, "The Bible says that those of us who sow among us should reap from us, that's implying that preachers should be taken care of."[35] Perhaps it's an unfair comparison, a Puritan's words against those of a flashy evangelical pastor from California. Or maybe the comparison presents a clear picture of just how much America's God has changed in the last four hundred years, how much we've fattened him up with materialisms, humanisms, individualisms, and Americanisms.

. . .

God's Spirit is all the rage in today's American culture. Americans make huge proclamations with God's Spirit. Some Americans cast out sex demons using the power of God's Spirit. No doubt the Holy Spirit is the most overused and misused member of America's Godhead. In a little more than one hundred years, America's charismatic movement has become one of the fastest-growing Christian movements in the United States and the fastest-growing Christian movement around the world.

Critics, Christian and otherwise, have voiced their strong opinions and fears about the doctrines of America's Holy Ghost movement, often declaring its teachings to be godless, unbiblical, or devoid of any logic or reason whatsoever. But critique, even when it comes from other Christians, means very little to most Christian leaders, mostly because when you're convinced that you have God on your side, why would you ever listen or respond to your critics? It happens, of course, but those occasions are rare. But once while preaching "the Word" on the Trinity Broadcasting Network, Benny Hinn did respond to his critics, telling TBN's owner, Paul Crouch, and the live studio audience how tired he was of people suggesting that what he preached wasn't the Word of God. "You know," shouted Hinn, "I've looked for one verse in the Bible—I just can't seem to find it—one verse that says, 'If you don't like 'em, kill 'em....' I really wish I could find it.... Sometimes I wish God would give me a Holy Ghost machine gun. I'd blow your head off."[36] That explains many Americans' charismatic approach to the Holy Spirit. Far too often, it's an anything-goes metaphysical theology with a good portion of hocus-pocus that tells outlandish stories about God, stories that alter, shape, and defame the name of God.

CHAPTER TEN

ONE NATION UNDER GODS

Starting in 1979, everything about America's God led back to Jerry Falwell. America's God would likely not be the Almighty American without Falwell's grit and fortitude. To say that Falwell was a polarizing figure is an understatement, because sometimes the Baptist preacher and founder of Liberty University was so divisive that his public persona became the apotheosis of the Christian stereotype, an ideal representative of everything that people love and hate about God in America.

George Marsden called Falwell the quintessential American fundamentalist, the kind who wore the title like a badge of honor, showcasing his allegiance to being a "separatist Baptist dispensationalist."[1] The key to American fundamentalism is "living separately." That's why the Puritans came to the New World, and that's why Jerry Falwell preached the Gospel of Politics to his followers, in the hope of creating a separate idea that could be enforced on all.

The American media loved Jerry Falwell. Most of them vehemently disagreed with him on air, but secretly they loved him. How could they not? He was ratings gold. Falwell served up his wild opinions with a kind of conviction that demanded response and almost always fit concisely into delightful thirty-second soundbites. Most journalists can't help but love a religious commentator who is ballsy enough to compare Hillary Clinton to Satan, antagonistic enough to suggest that the purple Teletubby is gay, and insensitive enough to blame the terrorist attacks of 9/11 on America's abortionists, feminists, and LGBTQ communities.

Politicians, pundits, and news anchors who knew Falwell personally often speak of him as having had a gentle spirit, a great sense of humor, and a character that in many ways belied his public persona. *New York* magazine's Kevin Roose was one of the last journalists to interview the preacher. As an undercover student at Liberty University, writing a memoir about being an "unlikely disciple" at the conservative university, Roose expected to hate the man whose "Gospel" defined the very rigid and less than open-minded Liberty environment. And while Roose disagreed with Falwell on a host of issues, political, religious, and social, he liked him personally. "Dr. Falwell wasn't a phony," Roose writes. "I liked his compassion among his people...his prankster streak...[and] that he made me question my own assumptions."[2] But even though Falwell was known to be friendly, that doesn't negate the fact that he promoted a God who loved the world so much that he planned to send roughly 93 percent of its population to hell.

And while Jerry Falwell's divisive persona reflects one part of his influence on God, there was another side of the fiery preacher, a unifying personality standing right in the middle of God's American universe.

. . .

As polarizing as Jerry Falwell's Christian messages were when he appeared as God's pundit, within the American Christian culture he was a unifying figure, one who helped merge the major forces of America's twentieth-century God—fundamentalism, evangelicalism, Catholicism, and Pentecostalism—to form a most influential spiritual and political force. Using Christian morality and the right-wing agenda as common denominators, Falwell forged a union, a sometimes volatile one, that amalgamated some of God's most conservative influencers and altered how America understood God, pursued God, and presented God in the late twentieth and early twenty-first century.

In 1978, singing groups from Liberty toured the country, preparing the way for "Jerry Falwell" and "America" to become synonymous ideas in the minds of Christians. I was five years old when the LBC Singers came and performed their *Look Up, America* cantata at my church, and I thought their hourlong patriotic-porn routine was unbelievable. Sunday nights after church, my family faithfully watched Falwell's *Old-Time Gospel Hour*, so I became well acquainted with his love for our country. His choir sang about America. His favorite singer, Robbie Hiner, crooned about America. Whenever he begged viewers for money, nearly every one of the free gifts people received when they donated fifty dollars or more was an American/God combo trinket that appeared to be made in Thailand. Rarely a week went by when he didn't mention America five or seventy-five times in a sermon.

In the late 1970s, Falwell started crisscrossing America, performing crusades, preaching the good news of America. While his message didn't change, the titles—his "America Back to God," "I Love America," "Clean Up America," and "Moral Majority" tours, to name a few—changed often. Falwell also turned his "America" sermon into three different books—*America Can Be Saved*, *How to Clean Up America*, and *Listen, America!*—and several dozen Old-Time Gospel Hour publications.[3]

By the mid-1970s, Falwell was, along with other Independent Fundamental Baptist preachers like Curtis Hutson and Jack

Hyles, among fundamentalism's golden boys. Though his relationship with America's powerhouse fundies would begin to sour in 1980—that was the year he decided to join hands in the name of politics with Catholics, Pentecostals, and evangelicals—Falwell delivered a fiery sermon at several fundamentalist Baptist pastor conferences in 1976. That sermon detailed what Falwell was thinking at the time and foreshadowed his future aspirations.[4]

In an effort to build a "biblical case" that America was sick and needed his help, Falwell relied on a 1976 Gallup poll on America and religion. The poll found that 34 percent of the nation's adults professed to "being saved," or born again, which Falwell referred to as his forty-five to fifty million "grains of salt." In his sermon—this time called "Seven Things Corrupting America"—Falwell added twenty-five million "grains" to represent children under the age of eighteen. The way he saw it, seventy-five million Americans loved Jesus, and he believed it was his calling to rally this group together and create an unstoppable army of God.[5] But there were obstacles to making this a reality, and so Falwell preached:

> Those 75 million Americans...are a mighty force of God in this generation if properly taught, trained, and disciplined. I look on us preachers as that army of mobilizers and spiritual organizers who have to go out like the labor union and find them and bring them into our camp, teach them the Word of God, train them in the way of God, and set their souls on fire.[6]

When Falwell's American mission began, it was packaged as a fundamentalist Christian mission. It possessed all the necessary ingredients. Soul winning? Check. Bible teaching? Check. Set their souls on fire? Check. Train and discipline them? Check. But four years later, Falwell's mission would change. That's about the time when he began having regular conversations with some of America's most conservative religious leaders, a roster of names that included Tim LaHaye (the man who would one day become a multimillionaire coauthor of the Left Behind series), Oral Roberts (the Pentecostal favorite who would eventually lock himself up in a tower and demand his own $2 million ransom, and then blame God for his actions), and Jim Bakker (who would soon be indicted on eight counts of mail fraud, fifteen counts of wire fraud, and one count of conspiracy and found guilty on all twenty-four counts). The conversations these men were engaging in involved America's political woes. And considering the 1970s brought *Roe v. Wade*, Nixon's Watergate, high inflation, President Jimmy Carter, and more, these men had much to discuss.

When President Carter caught wind that conservative evangelicals were unhappy with his performance, he invited them to breakfast. That gathering didn't go well. For starters, Carter was a Democrat, and despite his Southern Baptist roots and his love for Jesus, by refusing to join Falwell and friends at the March for Life later that afternoon he made all of God's men angry. However, it was Carter's defense of the ERA—the Equal Rights Amendment, legislation that would guarantee equal rights to women—that sent Jerry, Tim, Jim, Oral, and others storming out of the meeting. As they left, Tim LaHaye stage-whispered a prayer: "God, we have got to get this man out of the White House."[7]

Then, like an epiphany from God, Jerry Falwell remembered the seventy-five million born-again Christians he'd been keeping in his back pocket for a rainy day. As far as he was concerned, that day had come. What if he and his buddies could mobilize God's American people under some kind of Christian ideal? What if he could cast a clear vision of how America should be, could be, would be, if...

Falwell believed that, if united, the born-again vote would control more than one-third of America's political power. Suddenly, finding his seventy-five million people Bible-believing churches, teaching them God's Word, and disciplining them was pushed to the back burner. Falwell had a better idea, an idea that might save the soul of America, and in 1979 the preacher formed the Moral Majority.

And God's story would begin to change once again. But before we can understand the future, we have to first revisit the decades that led us here.

. . .

Starting in 1947, a new American sweetheart rose on the religious scene: Billy Graham. His rise to fame was due at least in part to how he shaped the message of Jesus. While his doctrines were identical to those of the fundamentalist preachers who promoted God with hellfire and damnation, soon after his public ministry began, Graham started softening his approach to preaching the Gospel.

America's Christian history had molded Jesus into a white American superhero by the 1950s, one who possessed the same masculine qualities as the cultural heroes of the day. Prior to the 1880s, worshipers focused their attention primarily on God rather than Jesus. In most respects, Jesus was a sacrifice to satisfy God's anger and wrath, a divine means to an end. Later, after America's Christians got to know Jesus and started making him the focus of Christianity, preachers and teachers in the late 1800s and early 1900s began sermonizing and theologizing about Jesus's humanity as much as his divinity.

When Billy Graham came along, there were two Americanized Jesuses. For some, Jesus was an Anglo-Saxon, blue-eyed, John Wayne/Marlboro Man hybrid Super Savior, and for others he was an olive-complexioned saintly and gentile middle-aged man with long, perfectly conditioned hair and quite obviously a virgin. Graham's Jesus was somewhere in the middle, a God-man whose masculine qualities were Jesus as God, strong, wise, good, merciful, and loving—*and* Jesus as human, understanding of the struggles of humanity, emotions, temptations, limitations, and dreams. Graham's Jesus wasn't too Baptist and he wasn't too Episcopalian but rather a balanced American savior who stood against the evils of the world as well as the evils in the personal lives of Americans.

Americans of all denominations and creeds fell in love with Billy Graham's Jesus. A revivalist as opposed to a church pastor, Graham found it easy to wow people with a relatable, down-to-earth Jesus. Graham's sermons portrayed God in such a way that people didn't become offended by the Christian message. Moreover, they connected to his spirited pleas. By the late 1950s, as hundreds of thousands became caught up in the Billy Graham craze, God's popularity in America began to surge. Of course, Graham was always quick to give God the glory in interviews and press conferences. But it was clearly not just God. Lots of evangelists, some far more talented at preaching than Graham, failed to build anything remotely close to his rapport with the American public. But that was his genius; he not only understood people, he was also humble enough to grow and learn from those around him and also from his audience.

In 1960, historian Sydney Ahlstrom wrote that "a brief consideration of Billy Graham is in order, for upon his manly shoulders has rested the burden of reviving mass evangelism and preventing it from becoming only a cheap and emotional accommodation of vague American yearning or a sentimental reversion to a not-so-old 'old-time religion.' Not significantly realized, however, is his solitariness in the field."[8] In other words, there was a great amount of pressure on Graham to do mass evangelism right. Which in many ways he did. Graham ignited America's heart with a true "evangelical" feeling, a hope-filled religious emotion that didn't rely so much on the Holy Spirit that non-Christians, Catholics, Episcopalians, Baptists, and Presbyterians were left squirming in their seats. While Graham wasn't the greatest preacher by many people's standards, it was difficult to deny the compassion and faith that enveloped his simple message. Plus, like D. L. Moody, his revivals and crusades paid homage to America's love for entertainment variety. Roger Bruns's biography of Graham describes the preacher's supporting cast of characters to include "impresarios, girl trios, magicians, huge choirs, swing-band instrumentalists, and even a horse named MacArthur who would kneel at the cross and tap 12 times, signifying the number of Christ's apostles. One memorable performance added a sonata for 100 pianos."[9]

. . .

How did Billy Graham change America's God? For one thing, he offered Americans a God that many found more conceivable than the one they knew or had heard about before, a God that was more involved and believable than the one Episcopalians talked about, more compassionate and less angry than the one Baptists preached about, and far less dramatic and orthodoxy-laden than the one Catholics taught about. In many ways, Graham's God was the peanut butter and jelly of Gods. Perhaps that was exactly what God needed at the time, to be presented in such a way that a wide variety of spiritual palates became delighted.

Regarding America's spirituality at the time, Sydney Ahlstrom writes that "the churches by and large seem to have done little more than provide a means of social identification to a mobile people." Ouch. But he's right in many ways. In the

1950s and 1960s, God was culture in America, like *The Tonight Show*, the Beatles, and *American Bandstand*. How one celebrated God defined a person into a statistical category, like race, nationality, marital status, and so forth.

Billy Graham shaped America's God by turning him into a package deal of "love," "mercy," and "eternity," making hell and damnation into sidebars, choosing to focus on what he believed really mattered to America's God. Graham's secret? "Sincerity is the biggest part of selling anything, including the plan of salvation."[10] And nobody believed Billy Graham's message more than Billy Graham.

Sincerity helped, but Graham was also in the right place at the right time. Like American culture at the time, his early ministry was defined by the Cold War. On more than one occasion Graham used his influence with God to promote an American Gospel, which for him was that "either communism must die, or Christianity must die, because it is actually a battle between Christ and anti-Christ."[11] Graham believed that the best answer to combating communism was Christianity, preaching on his radio program in the fall of 1953:

> Let us pray that if it be the will of God, that some day the Iron Curtain will be cracked for Christ and that the materialistic communism will be destroyed by the love, grace, and truth of the risen Christ....If that does not happen, these hydrogen bombs that can destroy whole cities and whole states with one blow may fall upon us in the next few years.[12]

During the Cuban Missile Crisis, Graham was performing a crusade in South America; even though he was supposed to be preaching Jesus to Argentinians, that hardly stopped him from calling the conflict "the prelude to the greatest crisis in the history of mankind" and criticizing America's policy to "compromise, talk, retreat, and appease."[13]

Politics did not hurt God's message. In fact, Graham used politics to energize America's need for God. By the mid-1960s, Billy Graham's ministry was the most powerful religious brand in the United States, and quickly becoming a spiritual force on the international stage as well.

. . .

Not all of America's Christians were sold on Graham's approach to God. While his God tasted sweet and was satisfying the spiritual hunger pains of everyday Americans, critics of the evangelist stood in all theological corners. Some thought Graham simplified God too much. Others thought he drained God of God. Still others believed he was theologically ignorant. But Graham's most vocal critics were those who believed he was too liberal. From their vantage point, God was far too important a topic to be muddied up with spiritual niceties like love, compassion, and grace or watered down with shenanigans like social reform, manners, and hope.

John R. Rice, the founder of America's go-to Bible-believing Baptist tabloid the *Sword of the Lord*, was Graham's chief defender early on. The *Sword* pronounced Graham "a powerful, spirit-filled, doctrinally sound young man."[14] But over time, Rice and Graham's friendship became strained, torn apart by their doctrinal differences, which were minor (and compared to where Graham ended up later in life, were hardly differences at all). But there were also politics involved. Every time Graham did something or said something that didn't sound like old-fashioned fundamentalism, Rice's phone would ring off the hook with fundamentalist preachers and apologists calling him to voice their concerns about Graham's wavering devotion to fundamentalism.

Rice sometimes took those concerns to Graham, and Graham would always assure his fundamentalist father figure that all was well with the world: He still believed in a hot hell, he still hated Catholics, and he still thought everybody who didn't agree with him was going to burn in hell. But that wasn't exactly true. And Graham knew it.

Personally, Rice may have been able to overlook the differences between him and Graham, but as America's reigning godfather of fundamentalism—with book sales in the millions, newspaper readership in the hundreds of thousands, and a pastoral influence comparable to Rick Warren's—John R. Rice could not just sweep the doctrinal differences under the rug. But Graham also had his future to think about. In order to fulfill his own "manifest destiny"—a reality that was quickly becoming as clear to his peers as it was to him—he could not be anchored down by ideas that he deemed petty compared to the individual great commission he was spearheading. For both men, their careers, legacies, and influences were at stake.

· · ·

Why was Billy Graham's friendship to John R. Rice so important? Because the companionship of Rice and Graham represented far more than just a close personal relationship; their bond also represented some of the last physical and relational strands holding together two movements, American fundamentalism and American evangelicalism.

Since 1942, America's fundamentalists and evangelicals had been united as members of the National Association of Evangelicals (NAE). The group's roster included John R. Rice, Bob Jones Sr., Billy Graham, David Otis Fuller, Carl F. H. Henry, Charles Woodbridge, J. Elwin Wright, Harold Ockenga, Leslie Roy Marston, Will Houghton, and a host of other conservative white American preachers. Even from the beginning this group was never quite the happiest of families, but they managed to stay together without any major blunders for ten or twelve years. But in 1956, that was all about to change. A Great Christian Divorce was coming, and neither Rice nor Graham could stop it.

The year following Rice and Graham's crusade in Scotland, Graham was quoted in *Christian Life* magazine as saying, "I can't call myself a fundamentalist."[15] And of course he couldn't, since the report went on to suggest that fundamentalism was laced with bigotry and narrow-mindedness. In 1956, Christians rarely whispered their discontent about angry hard-nosed believers, let alone said it bluntly in magazines. Still, Rice and Graham skirted the obvious for a few more months (their families even holidayed together in April 1956),[16] pretending that all was well with their friendship—and with the National Association of Evangelicals.

But weeks later, the calamity they were desperately trying to ignore became unavoidable. Rice wrote a scathing op-ed piece for the *Sword* about a number of NAE's members—among them Carl F. H. Henry and Harold Ockenga—suggesting that these "good Christian men" were actually "enlisted in a left-wing movement to bring in a 'new evangelicalism.'" Rice's piece concluded that "new evangelicals" had the audacity to "sneer at fundamentalists" and harp about "the reactionary anti-scholasticism of the fundamentalists of the past generation." Rice charged that these reckless Christians "[play] down fundamentalism and the defense of the faith, to poke fun at old-time fundamentalists, and to quote with glowing terms of appreciation the weighty pronouncements of infidel scholars."[17]

A few weeks after those words went public, Billy Graham announced that he was planning to launch a magazine called *Christianity Today*. And who did he hire as the periodical's premier editor? None other than one of the "fundamentalist sneerers," Carl F. H. Henry. Graham and Henry had met while studying at Wheaton College, and had known each other for years. Henry was a controversial choice not only because he was on the fundamentalists' watch list as a terror suspect, but because his book *The Uneasy Conscience of Modern Fundamentalism* had started a rift between the evangelicals and fundamentalists. In *Modern Fundamentalism*, Henry proclaimed that "fundamentalism is the modern priest and Levite, by-passing suffering humanity,"[18] suggesting that the very Christians that fundamentalists had called "the humanistic moralism of modern reformers"—in other words, the liberal Christ followers—were those whose faith gave them a purpose to feed the hungry, clothe the naked, and shelter the homeless. While Henry was hardly a liberal himself, he made no bones about calling fundamentalism ethically and socially irrelevant, obsessive about individual sins and silent on the world's evils, and crippled by its pessimistic eschatology.[19]

When Billy Graham chose the socially conscious Carl F. H. Henry to lead *Christianity Today*, that changed everything. Within months, Graham had resigned from the *Sword of the Lord*'s board of mostly preachers, and in the spring of 1957 Rice announced in the *Sword* that he could not support Graham's future revivals.[20] While God didn't exactly reach down from heaven with a pair of scissors and cut a line between America's Fs and America's Es, the effect was the same. Both men would later write about the ordeal. Rice defended his decision:

> I talked with Dr. Graham again and again about the danger of yoking up with modernism. Again and again he assured me that he had vowed to God he would never have a man on his committee who was not right on the inspiration of the Bible, the deity of Christ, and such matters....I wrote him in great detail on matters where I thought he was

wrong. And all the time I defended him openly and publicly, excusing his mistakes, until he openly declared he had decided to keep company with modernists and put them on his committees and to go under their sponsorship. Then I was compelled, in order to be true to Christ, to come out openly against that compromise.[21]

Graham also recalled the pain he felt:

Painful to me was the opposition from some of the leading fundamentalists [who] had been among our strongest supporters in the early years of our public ministry. Their criticism hurt immensely, nor could I shrug them off as the objections of people who rejected the basic tenets of the Christian faith or who opposed evangelism of any type. Their harshness and lack of love saddened me and struck me as being far from the spirit of Christ.[22]

Once the split became unofficially official, America's National Association of Evangelicals' God divided into two Gods, a God of American fundamentalism and a God of Billy Graham. Both Gods, along with America's emerging charismatic-healing, tongue-speaking, snake-handling drama God, would commune once more many years later in the name of politics. Each group would write different stories about God, stories that would affect every level of American society and forefront an effort to once again nationalize God and make America into the City Upon a Hill that John Winthrop had dreamed about nearly 350 years earlier.

. . .

In 1984, God was helping Curtis Hutson finish a new book. It was a doozy of a topic, even though it had been covered many times before. From Hutson's perspective, God was still mad as hell at those good-for-nothing "new evangelicals," the Christian movement that had been "new" for almost thirty years. And since God was angry, Hutson was angry too. Hutson believed that the "new evangelicals" were changing God. And since Hutson loved God, made his living by God, and was at the time considered one of the most prominent leaders of America's fundamentalist God, he needed to put his anger down on paper and publish it for other fundamentalists to read. Later that year his book—*New Evangelicalism: An Enemy of Fundamentalism*—was released. Hutson's book pronounced once again that fundamentalism was awesome and true, and that new evangelicalism was heretical, misguided, and not true. "Our responsibility is spiritual, not social," he declared early on, "but the New Evangelicals have become increasingly enamored with the liberal line of 'a social conscience.'"[23] And God forbid if Christians have consciences.

Curtis Hutson's biggest gripe was that evangelicals ignored the Apostle Paul's warning, "Wherefore come out from among them, and be ye separate." With that verse as his starting point, Hutson launched into a long-winded complaint. It was the same story, different generation. Fundamentalists believe that fundamentalists should only mingle with other fundamentalists.

For poor Hutson's sake, it's a good thing he died in 1995, long before Graham had the chance (in 2012) to meet with and then endorse a Mormon for president. More controversial still would have been Graham's comments in 2006 when he told *Newsweek* that "[in Jesus's] death on the cross, some mysterious thing happened between God and the Son that we don't understand. But there he was, alone, taking on the sins of the world....I spend more time on the love of God than I used to."[24] Those comments even made some evangelicals shiver, wondering if their onetime leader had grown closer to believing in "universal salvation" in his old age.

But in Hutson's defense, the man was only doing what fundamentalists had always done: stay on message. At its root, in addition to being separate from everybody who isn't fundamentalist, fundamentalism is about staying on and repeating one general message. That's what D. L. Moody did. That's what Billy Sunday did. That was what Billy Graham had once done. And that's what John R. Rice, Hutson's mentor, did. Which is why Hutson wrote the book. Because he'd been called by God and Rice to remain faithful to, above all things, the fundamentalist message.

Its supporters fight the same battles over and over and over again. This has been true since the 1920s, when the word "fundamentalist" was first coined to describe the militant faithful who had stopped evolving. The delusional part about fundamentalism is that many of those who adhere to it believe they live by a moral, ethical, and lifestyle code that originated in the days of John the Baptist. That's why many of them, the non-Calvinists, at least, don't call themselves Protestants, because they don't believe the term applies to them, insisting that they're above the world's secular labelings of religiosity. However, the majority of their doctrines are no more than 100 or 150 years old, so their "biblical roots" are pretty unfounded. But that's the message they've been taught. And that's why they repeat it.

Perhaps staying on message is important to fundamentalists because they believe that God is glorified by hearing them state their case over and over again. While today's fundamentalism comes in a variety of denominations and theologies—from Baptist to Pentecostal to Presbyterian, from Dispensationalism to Calvinism to Holy Spiritism—what argument do most fundies still spend a good deal of time harping about? *Evolution.* Fundamentalists will champion against evolution and promote creationism or intelligent design, as many call it today, until their dying breath because, sadly, much of their belief system depends on fighting that fight. For many, that's the whole of their faith, *the fight*. The majority of Christians who live and die on the Adam and Eve story from the Book of Genesis being historically true do so because if it isn't true, it casts doubt or discrepancy on the majority of their doctrinal beliefs as well as their understanding of scripture. They call this the "slippery slope," an idea that suggests biblical inerrancy must be believed in whole, because if one verse or story in the Book of Genesis isn't factually true, then what's stopping a person from suggesting that a story in the Book of Ezekiel or a detail in the Gospel of Matthew or a doctrinal stance in the Second Book of Corinthians isn't true?

And that's why staying on message is of such grave importance. Because the Bible's inerrancy is the foundation on which many Christians—fundamentalists, evangelicals, and others—build their entire faith upon. Because they need it. And they believe there's glory to be gleaned in repeating their assumed biblical truth over and over again. That's why they shout their messages on street corners, troll their messages online, or load YouTube clips of them declaring their messages publicly. There is glory in "the fight," in the preaching of their "truth" over and over again to their choir, church, or supporter. They are like peacocks, spreading their feathers wide and strutting around to pontificate their truths among other peacocks. Because again, *the fight* is the crux of the fundamentalist's faith.

. . .

How did such a strict, all-consuming faith survive an American culture that was becoming more and more enlightened by the decade? A few factors played into America's love affair with fundamentalism's God. First of all, America's culture in the

1960s—the sexual revolution, the civil rights movement, President Kennedy's assassination, the boom of Hollywood and live television coverage, the rise of "rock and roll," baby boomers coming of age, and America's engagement in the Vietnam War—created a ripe environment for Christian fundamentalism to spawn out of control. For so many, religious and nonreligious alike, America was in turmoil. And the 1970s weren't any better. The cultural landscape of these decades could not have offered a more perfect backdrop for America's fundamentalist God. What better way to introduce a God who was preparing to unleash the End of Time than against a cultural narrative that seemingly could be perceived as the end of time? The words that fundamentalists preached in regard to God and what was to come could easily be sensed as "truth" since America seemed to be preparing to take a swan dive off the crazy cliff and into a reality that could easily be spun as "the Seven-Year Tribulation." Even though America had encountered End-like decades before—World War I, the Great Depression, and World War II—the 1960s and 1970s offered a more tangible and hopeless narrative thread—one they could watch over and over again on their televisions—that those past apocalyptic years did not.

Many could sense a moral decline, especially considering that liquor was legal again and the theory of evolution was finding inroads into our educational system. However, our domestic sins had not yet contaminated America's pride and the common belief that, despite our mess, our intentions were good. Also, the overall assumption during the world wars was that fighting those battles was justified because we were fighting such innate evil that our losses would ultimately make the world better. The Vietnam War didn't offer such a story line, at least not as a whole. Between 1965 and 1971, America's belief that "Vietnam" was a mistake increased from roughly 40 to 72 percent.[25] Combine our inability to comprehend the moral justice of fighting in a war with the very palpable realization that, considering our growing infatuation with sex, drugs, alcohol, rock and roll, and other sins, America might not be "good" after all, it's somewhat easy to understand why fundamentalism became a logical answer to our country's problems. The other reason America's "sins" seemed ever-present was television. America wasn't just reading about the dirty deeds that happened in Hollywood or during rock concerts, we were also seeing footage of those moments on television. Big events and tragedies—President Kennedy's funeral, for instance—became experiences that, for the first time, Americans engaged in together as one big community. That technology allowed Americans to become sad, angry, happy, and filled with tears of joy all at the same time for exactly the same reasons.

In some ways, America was seeing—*really* seeing—America for the first time. And most didn't like what they saw. What better response was there than to find retreat among a religious sect that offered not only spiritual connection and biblical community but also a lifestyle that was going to, for better or worse, give their teenagers something "moral" to do on Friday nights? America's God of fundamentalism made a lot of sense. What's more, many people needed and wanted quick spiritual fixes, and if there's any area of religion that fundamentalists have perfected, it's God's quick fix. And in those days, even the most distant Christian could experience a quick "conversion" or "rededication" by reciting a prayer, getting a haircut, and making a few wardrobe adjustments.

Throughout the 1960s and 1970s, God's most conservative Bible thumpers flourished, especially in America's South. Though Rice's and Hutson's denominational flavor happened to be Baptist, fundamentalism bred among many of America's denominations, from charismatic-flaired Churches of God to the more Baptist-like congregations of Churches of Christ.

A key reason fundamentalism possessed such deep generational roots in the South was its close association with the fight against civil rights. As America's black churches began rallying for equal rights under the law, some of the movement's chief opposition came from the backwoods theologies of some of America's white churches. In 1963, God in America was still a long way off from being color-blind. Not all fundamentalist churches opposed the civil rights movement, but few supported it. Dr. Martin Luther King Jr. once said, "Our lives begin to end the day we become silent about things that matter."[26] But that's exactly what many churches did; rather than taking sides via press releases, they took sides by remaining silent. Others vocalized their opposition with delight. In the *Southern Presbyterian Journal*, which became one of many media forums for those who fought against desegregation, the journal's founder, L. Nelson Bell, argued that even though some followers of Jesus supported integration, "There are others—and they are as Christian in their thinking and practice as any in this world—who believe that it is un-Christian, unrealistic, and utterly foolish to *force* those barriers of race which have been established by God and which when destroyed by man are destroyed to his own loss."[27] Pentecostal-leaning denominations remained largely silent on race-related issues. Though the Assemblies of God and Church of God released vague statements trying to toe the line between race-conflicted parishioners, neither denomination was in a hurry to ban segregation among their communities of believers. Many Southern Baptists fought against the march for equality, its members working against the movement in and out of the spotlight, vehemently opposing and throwing up blockades to avoid desegregation.

Even the Christians who seemed slightly merciful to the cause of Dr. Martin Luther King and others walked the line between supporting civil rights and losing the financial giving of their parishioners who opposed it. One of those men—L. Calvin Bacon, an Assemblies of God minister from Atlanta—seemed to try to straddle both sides of the issue. After the assassination of Dr. King, Bacon felt compelled to attend the civil rights leader's funeral. Later he wrote that while he didn't approve of "Dr. King's activities," he had attended his funeral to protest the violence of his murder. Summing up his thoughts, Bacon expressed, "While we deplore the violence that racial unrest has brought to our land, we who know the Lord and His Word must recognize that the spreading revolution and lawlessness are part of the divine judgement. Sins of omission are just as serious as sins of commission."[28] That said, Bacon concluded that "the Civil Rights legislation cannot, I believe, meet the basic needs of our ghettos, but the gospel can."[29] Evangelical Christians were only slightly more progressive in their support of Civil Rights.

Billy Graham walked the line too. Though he counted Dr. King a personal friend, one whom he met at a 1957 crusade in New York City, when it came to rallying support around King's cause, Graham chose his actions carefully, with the mastery of a politician. On one hand, Graham never segregated his revivals. But when he was invited to march with Dr. King in Washington, D.C., in 1963, he declined. In a letter to President Eisenhower, he wrote, "I feel with you that the Church must take a place of spiritual leadership in this crucial matter that confronts not only the South but the entire nation" and yet he urged his presidential friend—"particularly before November," as he was up for reelection—to "stay out of this bitter racial situation that is developing."[30]

Dr. King praised Graham for his support, going as far as to say that "my work in the civil rights movement would not have been as successful as it has been" without him. And yet Graham seemed less than confident that anything good would come from the movement, once saying that "only when Christ comes again will the little white children of Alabama walk hand in hand with little black children."[31]

Honestly, it's difficult to peg Graham's role in the civil rights movement. Some historians have portrayed his involvement as heroic, that he was a champion for the cause. More recently, others have painted that influence in more indifferent, perhaps cowardly shades of gray. Perhaps both depictions offer truth, and yet neither is alone the whole truth. Graham certainly used his influence to move the cause forward, and he probably could have used it more. But no matter how one colors his racial initiatives—whether he's a leader who fought to open up the eyes of America's clergy or the man who used his influence and political savvy to sway America's opinions about race and equality—how sad is it that a large percentage of America's church, though nearly one hundred years removed from the Civil War, was still using the Bible and God and that hideous urban legend regarding Noah's son Ham to defend their prejudices against people of color? Even today, though America's church has made hopeful strides toward bringing diversity to its congregations, the majority of us still attend churches that are largely segregated on racial lines. Though most of us believe in racial equality, a devotion reflected in nearly every area of our lives, that devotion has never fully transcended the lines Americans draw in how we worship God.

•   •   •

During the second half of the twentieth century, America's evangelical God would become defined mostly by the work of Billy Graham. In some ways, America's evangelical God *was* Billy Graham. That's not to say that other evangelical ideas that came together after the Great Split lacked importance or didn't move God's story along—indeed, many did—but from 1955 to 1995, few people, ministries, or ideas came as close to impacting God's evangelical nature in America as Graham did. And while Graham's greatest and most influential achievement might be his role as America's pastor—perhaps the most influential American preacher of all time—I believe his greatest impact on the American story of God was *not* what he did when he was behind the pulpit and in front of thousands. I think Billy Graham's most influential role in shaping God came from the Christian enterprise he erected when he wasn't preaching.

I'm not trying to undermine Graham's preaching and message, but like the American evangelists before him—from George Whitefield to D. L. Moody to Billy Sunday—Graham was more than just a famous American preacher. Because the whole time Billy Graham was preaching the Gospel of God to America, Billy Graham™ was helping to fulfill the Great American Commission of GOD®.

And by GOD®, it was good—very good. The people who steered Billy Graham's ministry from behind the scenes exalted not only Christ but also Graham, making him America's first ministry tycoon. At the urging of his ministry supporters, Graham incorporated the Billy Graham Evangelistic Association (BGEA), which turned Billy Graham™ into one almighty media brand. Graham's mission? *Make Jesus famous by every means available.* And that they did. And by default, wherever the name of Jesus was uplifted, so too was the name of Billy Graham. His name became one of the most recognized and loved in American history, and his brand turned into a commodity that launched a Graham-inspired media empire leading to a host of opportunities. In time, BGEA's impact could be heard, seen, read, and experienced through radio, television, movies, publishing, books, and a myriad of other Jesus- and Billy-focused products. Since 1955, Graham's face has appeared on Gallup's Most Admired list a whopping fifty-five times. Though Graham's personal goal was always to make the name of Jesus known, it was his own name that turned into a proprietary item that launched the careers of preachers, politicians, singers, musicians, authors, speakers, media personalities, and businesspeople.

While it is unclear whether or not Billy Graham is to blame for the invention of the generic Christian T-shirt, the introduction of the American Christian T-shirt most definitely evolved out of an evangelical culture that Billy Graham™ first cultivated, a culture where ministry, capitalism, and media merged into a holy American ménage à trois. That threesome created an environment that not only helped to sell God and a host of God-branded products in America and around the world, but also created GOD®, the brand above all brands. And even as Graham's health began to wane with age, eventually forcing the preacher into retirement, the part of his legacy that may live on forever is America's strong love for GOD® that he helped sew into the hearts and minds of America's evangelicals.

Of course, Graham didn't create GOD® alone. Sooner or later, GOD® turned into a divine entity all its own. And today, GOD® has become so infused into every aspect of America's culture—from church and ministry to nonprofits and politics to social justice and social media to self-help concepts and point-of-purchase trinkets—that most people have become so accustomed to GOD® that we're incapable of differentiating God's presence from GOD®'s presents, or God's peace from one of GOD®'s piece-of-crap products made in Indonesia. A majority of Americans have become convinced that God and GOD® are synonymous. In many ways, they are the same being, a deity and brand morphed perfectly together for our good.

Perhaps the most powerful function of GOD® is its ability to be everything that God cannot be or has chosen not to be. Because unlike God, GOD® can do just about anything. GOD® can be merchandised, politicized, modernized, and super-sized.

GOD® can make lofty promises, offer interest rates, make life miserable for gay people, and abduct small children and take them on tours of heaven. GOD® can offer courses on raising dead people, project daily prophecies about the Middle East, declare President Obama to be the Antichrist, and micromanage the egos of megachurch pastors. GOD® can overlook sexual abuse inside churches, limit the national, spiritual, and communal rights of women, join Chick-fil-A in a war against marriage equality, and erect a fake Noah's Ark somewhere in Kentucky. GOD® can be printed, embroidered, 3-D'd, and reduced to fit inside a snow globe. GOD® puts doctrine before people, legislation before people, theology before people, and laws before people. GOD® can be created, refashioned, edited, and manipulated into our own image and used however we see fit.

Billy Graham didn't mean to create GOD®. There was no way he could know that mixing a deity with the capitalistic ideals of a successful, thriving democracy would evolve into something otherworldly, an idol that America's evangelical culture worships alongside God. Today, many of America's Christians are trying to sort through what is GOD® and what is God, a narrative that will be a part of America's God for many years to come.

• • •

By 1981, Jerry Falwell had successfully turned God into America's most powerful political influence. Before rallying together under the Moral Majority, Christians in America felt politically powerless, failing to realize just how many elections they could control if they worked together. Having already promoted its role in helping Ronald Reagan win the 1980 presidential election, Falwell believed even bigger election returns were possible. After cutting off evangelical support for President Carter, the incumbent, Falwell anticipated helping President Reagan lead the country back to 1950 or any year when abortion was illegal, when everybody hated homosexuality as much as Falwell, and equal rights still didn't include women.

America's God had his work cut out for him in the 1980s and 1990s. Humanism was roaming around like a lion, growling about on television and on Capitol Hill, and it had been spotted more than a few times in America's heartland eating children. Humanism was a massive problem, an evil problem, and for the leaders of America's evangelical elite, the perfect problem. Juxtaposed against America's emerging MTV generation, the Democrats' liberal (and seemingly outrageous) agendas, and the growing international drama between the United States and the former Soviet Union—the Stars Wars program, for example—humanism was a very sellable "evil" among people who loved Jesus and President Reagan. And adding the adjective "secular" as a modifier turned it into *secular humanism*, a term (coined in the 1950s) that became an unstoppable campaign for America's fear-filled evangelical administrators. That was how Falwell united America's Christians, by putting in front of them one humongous enemy that could only be beaten if Christians—all moral-minded Christians—worked together. For further effect, Falwell and associates added a healthy dose of fear to their messaging (*It is everywhere!*) leaving just enough mystery (*It might be sitting beside your child right now in science class!*)—to urge an immediate and proactive response.

Secular humanism became evangelical America's new Satan. Which was great for Christian leaders, because many believed that America needed a new Satan. Among the general public, belief in Satan was on the decline, most people only thinking Lucifer existed in jokes and occasionally in skits on *Saturday Night Live*. But the real issue regarding Satan was that even among Christians, people who believed in the devil's existence and power, few felt threatened by the "Evil One," at least not enough to do anything about the menace. While most knew or assumed Satan was out there somewhere—they'd seen pictures of Ozzy Osbourne and Alice Cooper, after all—many were convinced that he didn't pose a real threat to their livelihood. But Falwell changed all of that. America's lobbying pastor resurrected Satan from the dead, gave him a new name—*secular humanism*—and positioned "him" in such a way that every born-again Christian could look around and see for themselves his very real presence in their American lives.

Falwell's plan was, among Christians anyway, genius. What better way to rally the troops than to offer them a common threat, something that likely existed on their bookshelves inside their homes? Soon everybody was talking about "secular humanism," and not only that, but most were beginning to see symptoms of it in their schools, local governments, television programming, at the movies, and sometimes even working its way inside their churches.

Falwell didn't sell the idea alone, of course. All of his white friends joined the campaign. In his book *Battle for the Mind*, Tim LaHaye defined humanism, believing that the best way to sell the evil was to make it real. And LaHaye did just that: He used scripture, stories, and historical events to fashion secular humanism into a crafty little demon, one that breaks into homes undetected and, rather than abducting children, just takes their brains. While LaHaye admitted that the number of humanists living in America wasn't large, he warned that Christians should not underestimate them because nearly all of them were college-educated and working in highly influential positions in "government, public schools, TV, and pornographic-literature sources," their mission was "anti-God, anti-moral, anti-self-restraint, and anti-American," and their number one goal was to "destroy the family."[32] LaHaye was convincing, too, because he made secular humanism the main cause of the world's problems, writing that it was "why humanist politicians permitted Russia to conquer the satellite countries of Europe and turn them into socialist prisons."[33] And he didn't stop there, either. According to LaHaye, secular humanism was why we failed to win the Korean War and the Vietnam War, and why we lost the Panama Canal. It was also the root cause of why Cuba became a satellite country of the U.S.S.R., complete with submarines and three thousand troops.[34] Though it sounds like another one of those shows on the CW, this was not fiction according to Falwell and his pals. What they were fighting was as real as the Holy Spirit, according to those leading the attack.

And politically that's just what it was, an attack. Falwell's Moral Majority became, for a short ten years, a mighty force of evangelical power to fight secular humanism. While it never became the force that Falwell had envisioned, it likely accomplished more than many realize. Most influential? It empowered Christians to become a political force. While not every Christian group or leader joined Falwell's "Majority," most did join his fight.

Though they loved President Reagan, and no doubt helped to secure his massive landslide victory in 1984, Reagan failed Christians in several respects. He did nothing in regard to abortion. And he failed to put prayer back in public schools. Also, as Garry Wills explains, "true, [Reagan] gave them Antonin Scalia on the [Supreme] Court, and appointed many conservatives to lower-level federal benches. But he did not back the conservatives' Family Protection Act."[35] But Reagan's greatest *Moral* failure? He showcased some political compassion for AIDS victims.[36] God hated that, according to the conservatives in control of God at the time. However, despite setbacks, Christian conservatives spearheaded a political movement, a "born again" faith (with politics) that materialized as the Moral Majority, the Conservative Caucus, the Christian Broadcasting Network, Christian Voice, the Christian Coalition, the American Family Association, and Concerned Women for America. Christian groups that hadn't dabbled much in politics before—Focus on the Family and Campus Crusade for Christ, for starters—began playing on various levels in the Washington, D.C., craziness.

By the late 1980s, America's God had turned into a professional lobbyist, raging against anything and everything that Christians deemed appropriate for God to rage against, from gay rights to women's rights, from evolution to environmental pollution, from *The Last Temptation of Christ* to the Smurfs—if it smelled like secular humanism, God brought his political wrath to the party. In 1988, God encouraged Pat Robertson to run for president. Despite Robertson's suggesting that it was God's will for him to become president, he lost. Regarding who won, Robertson later wrote in his 1992 book *The New World Order* that George H. W. Bush (among others) was "in reality unknowingly and unwittingly carrying out the mission and mouthing the phrases of a tightly knit cabal whose goal is nothing less than a new order of the human race under the domination of Lucifer and his followers."[37]

In 1991, God began rallying against the presidential hopes of Bill and Hillary Clinton. That didn't go so well. Two years later, God helped secure the support of Christians for Newt Gingrich's "Contract with America." It's unclear why God supported Gingrich's plan, considering the contract didn't necessarily offer Christians any political kickback. In 1996, not even God believed that Bob Dole was a good presidential candidate or capable of beating Bill Clinton. By 1999, many among the Christian right were becoming discouraged. Among them was an early supporter of Jerry Falwell's Moral Majority, Paul Weyrich. "We got our people elected, but that did not result in the adoption of our agenda." Weyrich's plan was to leave the political scene and retreat to a quiet spot where he planned to live a "godly, righteous, and sober" life.[38]

. . .

With a little help from the Supreme Court, God helped George W. Bush get elected as president of the United States in 2000. The Christian support for Bush was large, considering he'd promised America's evangelicals that his decision-making question was this: "What would Jesus do?"[39] And while the answers to that question would include a host of presidential actions that many Christians didn't think Jesus would ever do, the majority of America's evangelical forces remained true to Bush's dream that America was a true light, one that "shined in darkness and the darkness did not overcome it." Throughout his presidency, Bush spoke often of America's "light," once calling our country "the brightest beacon for freedom and opportunity in the world."

As America's first true evangelical Christian president in more than fifty years, a politician with ties to all of Christianity's big names, from Billy Graham to Ted Haggard, W. helped bring the merging of faith, politics, patriotism, and prophecy back to the forefront of the American conversation. Much like William McKinley, Bush felt called to his position as president. His role as national comforter after 9/11—an occasion that swelled his approval ratings well into the 80th percentile—only strengthened that belief, eventually leading him on a mission from God to "rid the world of the evil-doers."[40] Bush's Christian fan base applauded the president's divine sensibilities. Prominent Christian radio pundit Janet Parshall declared, "I think that God picked the right man at the right time for the right purpose."[41] Eighteen months later, when Bush turned his eyes toward Iraq, Christians supported the military action, many deeming it the ultimate war of Good versus Evil. The Christian newsmagazine *World* went so far as to proclaim that "Saddam's regime has been not only anti-democratic but Satanic in its treatment of human beings."[42] Leading up to Bush's reelection in 2004, General William Boykin, one of the men leading the search for Osama bin Laden, toured churches, donning combat gear and featuring a slideshow presentation. One of his points included:

Ask yourself this: why is this man in the White House? The majority of Americans did not vote for him. Why is he there? I tell you this morning he's in the White House because God put him there for such a time as this. God put him there to lead not only this nation but to lead the world in such a time as this.[43]

And who was America fighting, again? According to General Boykin, it wasn't bin Laden or Saddam Hussein. "The battle this nation is in is a spiritual battle," said Boykin, "it's a battle for our soul. And the enemy is a guy called Satan....[Satan] wants to destroy us as a nation, and he wants to destroy us as a Christian nation."[44] Publicly, Bush distanced himself from the general's comments, which caused some of the president's diehard evangelicals to become perturbed with their leader. James Dobson called Boykin a true "martyr" and chided those who critiqued the war hero.

Still, despite the squabble, evangelicals came out in droves to support President Bush's reelection campaign. They had to. Americans, even many Christian Americans, had grown tired of fighting "Satan" in Iraq and were ready to jump ship to support "anybody but Bush." God's War became the topic that Americans would debate all the way up until election day. However, once the votes were counted, God, Bush, and America's evangelicals would continue fighting Satan for another four years.

At some point during George W. Bush's second term, America's God started leaning left. Christians started criticizing Bush's politics and his administration's policies. They started questioning and criticizing the war. Some evangelicals joined the fight to save the planet from global warming. By 2007, there were very real signs that Bush's presidency was hurting the Republican cause among younger evangelicals. One poll found that only 40 percent of young evangelicals identified as Republican, down from 55 percent two years earlier.[45]

Was God's American story once again beginning to change?

Jerry Falwell hoped that wasn't the case. Thirty-some years earlier, God had given Falwell strict "instructions regarding taking the Christian worldview to the public square." Which was what he believed he was doing. Falwell continued, "I have a calling from God: I utilize the secular media because I feel a personal calling and Divine enablement to confront the culture."[46] One thing is certain: The Lynchburg pastor never stopped offering his stern critiques of culture in America. In the last two months of 2006 alone, despite his popularity having taken a huge hit in recent years, Falwell took his message to news networks—CNN, MSNBC, NBC, Fox News, and C-SPAN— twelve different times. In the spring of 2007, CNN's Christiane Amanpour visited Falwell at Liberty University to interview him for a news special called *God's Warriors*. "We're trying to force God out of the public square, the public schools, our public lives," Falwell claimed. Regarding the American values he'd spent thirty years fighting for, he said, "My children are more likely to see this victory won than I am. I think we're fifty years away. We've got to stay with it, stay with it, stay with it and never give up."

One week later, Jerry Falwell died in his office on Liberty Mountain.

The following year, in a controversial move, Pastor Rick

Warren invited presidential candidates John McCain and Barack Obama to speak at his Saddleback Church in California. The evangelical pastor seemed to be making an intentional move toward evangelical nonpartisanship, a decision that a growing number of evangelicals seemed happy about. Not everybody was thrilled with Warren's move. And four years later, even Warren himself changed his political tune, coming out as a strong opponent to President Obama's second run for office. But in 2009, on the eve of Barack Obama taking the oath of office, Warren was still wearing his moderate hat. He even accepted Obama's offer to give the invocation at his inauguration. His prayer included the words:

> [God], History is your story. The Scripture tells us, "Hear O Israel, the Lord is our God. The Lord is One."...And as we face these difficult days ahead, may we have a new birth of clarity in our aims, responsibility in our actions, humility in our approaches, and civility in our attitudes, even when we differ....Help us to share, to serve and to seek the common good of all....May all people of goodwill today join together to work for a more just, a more healthy and a more prosperous nation and a peaceful planet. And may we never forget that one day all nations and all people will stand accountable before you.[47]

Rick Warren channeled a plethora of American Christianities in that inaugural prayer. At times he sounded as open-minded as an Episcopalian. Other times he seemed to let his inner dispensational evangelical shine more brightly. In quoting the Book of Deuteronomy and mentioning Israel, Warren sounded an awful lot like a Puritan.

As much as America has altered and shaped and added to God's story, some parts, for good and bad reasons, remain forever the same. As Warren said in his prayer, history tells God's story. And while that might sound like a statement about God, it's much more a statement about us, and the impact our lives, words, and stories have on the story of God in America. Just before they set sail on their journey for Boston, the Reverend John Cotton told the Puritans to heed Jesus's advice from the Gospel of Luke. "To whom much is given," he said, "of him God will require the more."

And if that was true then for the men and women telling America's story about God, how much more is required of those of us who share it now?

.   .   .

Maybe my friend Dave wasn't as crazy as I thought to wonder aloud where God would be without America. On more than a few occasions while writing this book, I too have caught myself wondering where God would be without the almighty United States. I've not only pondered *where*, but I've also wondered who God would be without this country. Of course, considering that we've been promoting, editing, and using God's story for his and our glory for nearly four hundred years, asking where and who he'd be without us is rather futile. That said, considering where and who America's God was in 1630 or in 1741 or in 1801 or in 1925 and in light of where and who America's God is today, I don't think it's futile for us to consider the weight and influence of our stories, beliefs, theologies, and ideas and to ponder how they might affect where and who America's God will be in the future. Because if our history is any indication, then God in America is bigger today than he was yesterday, and chances are he'll be bigger tomorrow than he was today. Because here in the United States of America, our God is great, our God is big, and our God is always growing.

ACKNOWLEDGMENTS

So many good people helped make this book possible. I'm grateful to Greg Daniel, my agent and friend, for believing in this project, my writing, and encouraging me to take literary risks. I'm also thankful for the passions, talents, and dedication of Wendy Grisham and Chelsea Apple, my champions and editors at Jericho Books. Without their hard work, this book wouldn't have happened. I'm also much indebted and grateful to the detailed editorial eye of Roland Ottewell. For believing in this book and for welcoming me into their publishing family with open arms, I want to thank all of the good people at Hachette Book Group.

For their encouragement, support, forgiveness, tolerance, and friendship, I am grateful to Adam Ellis, Matthew Costner, Rachel Held Evans, Ann Voskamp, Pete and Brandi Wilson, Elizabeth Esther, Todd and Angie Smith, Al and Leila Larson, Zack Hunt, Melissa Campbell, Curt and Brittany Anderson, Stephan Lamb, Brent and Tam Hodge, Jennifer Schuchmann, Sharideth Smith, Shawn Smucker, Jason Boyett, Rob Stennett, Michael Bianchi, Jon and Jenny Acuff, my "SFB family," and the social media team at World Vision.

I'm eternally grateful for my parents, Virgil and Carole Turner, and for my sisters, Melanie, Kelley, and Elisabeth, and their families; and also for my wife's family. For their laughter, pint-sized wisdom, and unconditional love, the gratitude I have in my heart for Elias and Adeline is more than words can describe. The joy of being their daddy is grace enough for each day. But above all, for her encouragement, love, mercy, sacrifice, and belief in me, my heart bursts with appreciation and love for my wife and closest friend, Jessica. Without her support and dedication, none of this would be possible.

NOTES

PROLOGUE

1   Gallup polling: Frank Newport, *God Is Alive and Well: The Future of Religion in America* (New York: Gallup Press, 2012), chapter 1.

2   Frank Newport, "In U.S., 77% Identify as Christian," Gallup Politics, December 24, 2012, http://www.gallup.com/poll/159548/identify-christian.aspx.

CHAPTER ONE: AN AMERICAN RESURRECTION OF GOD

1   James B. Finley, *Autobiography of Rev. James B. Finley; or, Pioneer Life in the West* (1853), ed. W. P. Strickland, 166, 362, 364.

2   Ibid., 366.

3   Ibid., 364.

4   Harold Bloom, *The American Religion: The Emergence of the Post-Christian Nation* (New York: Simon & Schuster, 1993), 61.

5   Governor John Winthrop, "A Model of Christian Charity," http://religiousfreedom.lib.virginia.edu/sacred/charity.html.

6   Francis J. Bremer, *John Winthrop: America's Forgotten Founding Father* (New York: Oxford University Press, 2003), 173.

7   John Cotton, "God's Promise to His Plantation," http://quintapress.macmate.me/PDF_Books/Gods_Promise_to_his_plantation.pdf.

8   Ibid.

9   Janice Knight, *Orthodoxies in Massachusetts: Rereading American Puritanism*, 157.

10 Sarah Palin, *America by Heart: Reflections on Family, Faith, and Flag* (New York: HarperCollins, 2010), 69.

11 Ronald Wilson Reagan, "Farewell Address (January 11, 1989), Miller Center, University of Virginia, http://millercenter.org/president/speeches/detail/3418.

12 In "A Model of Christian Charity," Winthrop cites from the Book of Micah, chapter six, verse eight: "He hath shewed thee, O man, what is good; and what doth the Lord require of thee, but to do justly, and to love mercy, and to walk humbly with thy God?"

13 Garry Wills, *Head and Heart: American Christianities* (New York: Penguin Press, 2007), 35.

CHAPTER TWO: THE TOTAL DEPRAVITY OF GOD

1   E. Brooks Holifield, *Theology in America: Christian Thought from the Age of the Puritans to the Civil War* (New Haven, CT: Yale University Press, 2003), 10.

2   Justin Taylor, "Rob Bell: Universalist?," The Gospel Coalition, February 26, 2011, http://thegospelcoalition.org/blogs/justintaylor/2011/02/26/rob-bell-universalist/.

3   2 Corinthians 11:14–15: "for Satan himself is transformed into an angel of light. Therefore *it is* no great thing if his ministers also be transformed as the ministers of righteousness; whose end shall be according to their works."

4   John M. Barry, *Roger Williams and the Creation of the American Soul: Church, State, and the Birth of Liberty* (New York: Viking Penguin, 2012), 220.

5   Selma R. Williams, *Divine Rebel: The Life of Anne Marbury Hutchinson* (1981), 110.

6   Roger Williams, *On Religious Liberty: Selections from the Works of Roger Williams*, ed. James Calvin Davis (Cambridge, MA: Belknap Press of Harvard University, 2008), 94.

7   Samuel Gardner Drake, *The History and Antiquities of the City of Boston* (1856), 226.

8   "A New Adam," *God in America*, PBS, http://www.pbs.org/godinamerica/transcripts/hour-one.html.

9   From Danforth's sermon "A Brief Recognition of New-Englands Errand into the Wilderness."

10 Perry Miller, *The New England Mind*, vol. 1, *The Seventeenth Century* (Cambridge, MA: Belknap Press of Harvard University), 77.

11 Edmund S. Morgan, *The Genuine Article: A Historian Looks at Early America* (New York: Norton, 2003), chapter 3, "Heaven Can't Wait."

CHAPTER THREE: GOD IN THE HANDS OF ANGRY PEOPLE

1   Bill Wiese, *23 Minutes in Hell: One Man's Story About What He Saw, Heard, and Felt in That Place of Torment* (Lake Mary, FL: Charisma House, 2006), 2–3.

2   Albert M. Winseman, "Eternal Destinations: Americans Believe in Heaven, Hell," May 25, 2004, Gallup, http://www.gallup.com/poll/11770/eternal-destinations-americans-believe-heaven-hell.aspx.

3   Thomas S. Kidd, *The Great Awakening: The Roots of Evangelical Christianity in Colonial America* (New Haven, CT: Yale University Press, 2007), Kindle edition, locations 148–49.

4   Ibid., locations 149–51.

5   Stephen Prothero, *American Jesus: How the Son of God Became a National Icon* (New York: Farrar, Straus and Giroux, 2003), Kindle edition, 43.

6   Kidd, *The Great Awakening*, locations 209–10.

7   Ibid., locations 215–16.

8   George M. Marsden, *Jonathan Edwards: A Life* (New Haven, CT: Yale University Press, 2003), Kindle edition, location 682.

9   Ibid., location 423.

10 Ibid., location 435.

11 Ibid., locations 423–24.

12 Ibid., locations 891–94.

13 Ibid., locations 673–74.

14 Ibid., locations 674–76.

15 Ibid., location 680.

16 Randall J. Peterson and Joel R. Beeke, *Meet the Puritans* (Grand

Rapids, MI: Reformation Heritage Books, 2006), Kindle edition, location 2987.

17 Jonathan Edwards, Henry Rogers, Sereno Edwards Dwight, *The Works of Jonathan Edwards, A.M.: With an Essay on His Genius and Writings, Volume 2* (1839), 911.

18 Marsden, *Jonathan Edwards*, locations 1835–36.

19 Ibid., locations 2219–20.

20 Ibid., location 2268.

21 Ibid., location 3061.

22 Ibid., locations 3069–70.

23 Ibid., location 3072.

24 Ibid., location 3083.

25 Ibid., locations 3104–5.

26 Ibid., locations 3109–10.

27 Jonathan Edwards, *Seeking God: Jonathan Edwards' Evangelism Contrasted with Modern Methodologies*, ed. William C. Nichols (Ames, IA: International Outreach, Inc., 2001), Kindle edition, locations 7688–89.

28 Sean Michael Lucas, *God's Grand Design: The Theological Vision of Jonathan Edwards* (Wheaton, IL: Crossway, 2011), 210.

29 Marsden, *Jonathan Edwards*, locations 3377–79.

CHAPTER FOUR: THE EVANGELICALS ARE COMING!

1 Stephen Prothero, *American Jesus: How the Son of God Became a National Icon* (New York: Farrar, Straus and Giroux, 2003), Kindle edition, 44.

2 Thomas S. Kidd, *The Great Awakening: The Roots of Evangelical Christianity in Colonial America* (New Haven, CT: Yale University Press, 2007), Kindle edition, location 712.

3 Ibid., location 731.

4 "A New Adam," *God in America*, PBS, http://www.pbs.org /godinamerica/transcripts/hour-one.html.

5 "George Whitefield," Christian History, http://www.christianitytoday .com/ch/131christians/evangelistsandapologists/whitefield.html.

6 Douglas Sweeney, *The American Evangelical Story: A History of the Movement* (Grand Rapids, MI: Baker Academic, 2005), Kindle edition, 42.

7 Ava Chamberlin, "The Grand Sower of the Seed: Jonathan Edwards's Critique of George Whitefield," *New England Quarterly* 70, no. 3 (September 1997): 368–85.

8 Kidd, *The Great Awakening*, location 708.

9 George Whitefield, *The Works of the Reverend George Whitefield* (1771–72), 297.

10 Kidd, *The Great Awakening*, locations 764–65.

11 Sweeney, *The American Evangelical Story*, Kindle edition, 49.

12 Ibid., 48.

13 Ibid., 56.

14 Ibid.

15 Ibid., 57.

16 Ibid.

17 Ibid., 58.

18 "A New Adam," *God in America*, PBS, http://www.pbs.org/godinamerica/transcripts/hour-one.html.

19 Thomas S. Kidd, *God of Liberty: A Religious History of the American Revolution* (New York: Basic Books, 2010), Kindle edition, locations 447–48.

20 Ibid., locations 449–50.

21 Mark A. Noll, *America's God: From Jonathan Edwards to Abraham Lincoln* (New York: Oxford University Press, 2002), Kindle edition, 76.

22 Ibid., 77.

23 Kidd, *God of Liberty*, 169.

24 Ibid., 169–70.

25 Ibid., 170.

26 Ibid., 50.

27 "A New Adam," *God in America*, PBS, http://www.pbs.org/godinamerica/transcripts/hour-two.html.

28 Garry Wills, *Head and Heart: American Christianities* (New York: Penguin Press, 2007), 189, 190.

29 Quoted in Marilyn Mellowes, "Jefferson and His Bible," *Frontline*, http://www.pbs.org/wgbh/pages/frontline/shows/religion/jesus/jefferson.html.

30 Mark A. Noll, *A History of Christianity in the United States and Canada* (Grand Rapids, MI: Eerdmans, 1992), Kindle edition, location 2238.

31 Darren Dochuk, *From Bible Belt to Sunbelt: Plain-Folk Religion, Grassroots Politics, and the Rise of Evangelical Conservatism* (New York: Norton, 2011), Kindle edition, location 323.

32 Ibid., locations 324–25.

33 Thomas Paine, *Common Sense* (1776), 20.

34 Noll, *America's God*, 84.

35 Ibid.

36 "Washington's Inaugural Address of 1789," http://www.archives.gov/exhibits/american_originals/inaugtxt.html.

37 Timothy Ballard, *The Covenant: One Nation Under God— America's Sacred and Immutable Connection to Ancient Israel* (New York: Legends Library, 2012), Kindle edition, locations 2176–78.

38 Wills, *Head and Heart*, 76.

CHAPTER FIVE: THE INDEPENDENCE OF GOD

1 Harold Bloom, *The American Religion: The Emergence of the Post-Christian Nation* (New York: Simon & Schuster, 1993), 59.

2 Rhodes Thompson, ed., *Voices from Cane Ridge* (Bloomington, MN: Bethany Press, 1954), 63.

3 Charles G. Finney, *The Memoirs of Rev. Charles G. Finney* (1876), 20.

4 Paul E. Johnson, *A Shopkeeper's Millennium: Society and Revivals in Rochester, New York, 1815–1837* (New York: Hill & Wang, 1978), 3.

5 Ibid.

6 Dr. Michael Horton, "The Disturbing Legacy of Charles Finney," Issues, Etc., http://www.mtio.com/articles/aissar81.htm#horton.

7 Thomas Jefferson to John Adams, April 11, 1823, reprinted in

The Reasoner, vols. 10–11, 50.

8   Mark A. Noll, *America's God: From Jonathan Edwards to Abraham Lincoln* (New York: Oxford University Press, 2002), Kindle edition, 167.

9   Garry Wills, *Head and Heart: American Christianities* (New York: Penguin Press, 2007), 288.

10   Noll, *America's God,* 200.

11   Roger E. Olson, *Arminian Theology: Myths and Realities* (Downers Grove, IL: InterVarsity Press, 2006), 103.

12   Peter Cartwright, *Autobiography of Peter Cartwright, the Backwoods Preacher* (1857), 110.

13   Ibid., 101.

14   Ibid., 79.

15   Stephen Prothero, *American Jesus: How the Son of God Became a National Icon* (New York: Farrar, Straus and Giroux, 2003), Kindle edition, 45.

16   Nathan O. Hatch, *The Democratization of American Christianity* (New Haven, CT: Yale University Press, 1989), 87.

17   David Hempton, *Methodism: Empire of the Spirit* (New Haven, CT: Yale University Press, 2005), 2.

18   Mark A. Noll, *A History of Christianity in the United States and Canada* (Grand Rapids, MI: Eerdmans, 1992), Kindle edition, location 2845.

19   Ibid., locations 2730–31.

CHAPTER SIX: THE DIVIDED STATES OF GOD

1   Molly Hennessy-Fiske, "Southern Baptists Oppose Scouting's Policy on Gays," *Los Angeles Times,* June 12, 2013, http://www.latimes.com/news/nation/nationnow/la-na-nn-baptists-boy-scouts-20130612,0,4980775.story.

2   "Wednesday SBC Meeting Blog," *Baptist Press,* June 11, 2013, http://baptistpress.com/BPnews.asp?ID=40486.

3   Tim Ellsworth, "Boy Scout Resolution Adopted by SBC," *Baptist Press,* June 12, 2013, http://bpnews.net/bpnews.asp?id=40499.

4   Greg Garrison, "Southern Baptist President Fred Luter Says His

Church Will Stop Hosting Boy Scouts After Vote to Accept Openly Gay Scouts," AL.com, June 15, 2013, http://www.al.com/living/index.ssf/2013/06/southern_baptist_convention_pr_1.html.

5   Irv A. Brendlinger, *To Be Silent... Would Be Criminal: The Antislavery Influence and Writings of Anthony Benezet* (Lanham, MD: Scarecrow Press, 2006), 102.

6   Ibid.

7   *New York Times*: http://www.nytimes.com/1860/07/09/news/the-slave-trade-an-original-letter-from-patrick-henry.html.

8   Albert Barnes, *The Church and Slavery* (1857), 62.

9   Edwin Scott Gaustad, *A Religious History of America*, 164.

10 Ibid., 168.

11 Ibid., 168–69.

12 Garry Wills, *Head and Heart: American Christianities* (New York: Penguin Press, 2007), 303.

13 Harriet Beecher Stowe, *Uncle Tom's Cabin* (1852), chapter 45.

14 Wills, *Head and Heart*, 337.

15 George M. Marsden, *Understanding Fundamentalism and Evangelicalism* (Grand Rapids, MI: Eerdmans, 1991), Kindle edition, 9.

16 Richard A. Harris and Daniel J. Tichenor, eds., *A History of the U.S. Political System: Ideas, Interests, and Institutions* (Santa Barbara, CA: ABC-CLIO, 2010), 91.

CHAPTER SEVEN: GOD'S AMERICAN FUNDAMENTALS

1   George M. Marsden, *Understanding Fundamentalism and Evangelicalism* (Grand Rapids, MI: Eerdmans, 1991), Kindle edition, 1.

2   "I See Things," YouTube, http://www.youtube.com/watch?v=aVyFyauE4ig#at=202.

3   Collin Hansen, "Pastor Provocateur," *Christianity Today*, September 21, 2007, http://www.christianitytoday.com/ct/2007/september/30.44.html

4   Mark A. Noll, *A History of Christianity in the United States and Canada* (Grand Rapids, MI: Eerdmans, 1992), Kindle edition, location 6252.

5   Ibid., locations 6252–55.

6   Ibid., locations 6258–60.

7   "Phoebe Palmer: The Mother of the Holiness Movement," *Newlife*, June 10, 2011, http://newlife.id.au/equality-and-gender-issues/phoebe-palmer/.

8   "The Holiness Movement," http://www.unitypublishing.com/NewReligiousMovements/NewBrianCharismatics.html.

9   Richard Wheatley, *The Life and Letters of Mrs. Phoebe Palmer* (1876), 83.

10 Ibid.

11 Frank Lambert, *Religion in American Politics: A Short History* (Princeton, NJ: Princeton University Press, 2008), Kindle edition, locations 1146–49.

12 Ibid., locations 1152–53.

13 Richard Kyle, *Evangelicalism: An Americanized Christianity* (New Brunswick, NJ: Transaction Publishers, 2006), 68–69.

14 Garry Wills, *Head and Heart: American Christianities* (New York: Penguin Press, 2007), 344.

15 Kyle, *Evangelicalism*, 69.

16 Wills, *Head and Heart*, 345.

17 D. L. Moody and Charles F. Goss, *Echoes from the Pulpit and Platform* (1900), 242.

18 Wills, *Head and Heart*, 344.

19 George M. Marsden, *Understanding Fundamentalism and Evangelicalism* (Grand Rapids, MI: Eerdmans, 1991), Kindle edition, 21.

20 George M. Marsden, *Fundamentalism and American Culture* (New York: Oxford University Press, 2006), 50–51.

21 David Riddle Williams, *James H. Brookes: A Memoir* (1897), 149.

22 Ibid., 151.

23 "Founders Journal," Founders Ministries, http://www.founders.org/journal/fj09/article1.html.

24 Wills, *Head and Heart*, 360.

25 Vincent J. Schodolski, "Apocalypse How," *Chicago Tribune*, April 13, 2005, http://articles.chicagotribune.com/2005-04-13/news/

0504130178_1_evangelicals-moral-majority-rapture-index.

26 Cord Jefferson, "More Than 40 Percent of Americans Believe the Rapture Is Coming," *Good*, May 20, 2011, http://www.good.is/posts/more-than-40-percent-of-americans-believe-the-rapture-is-coming.

27 Robert Norton, *Memoirs of James & George Macdonald of Port-Glasgow* (1840), 171–176.

28 Barbara R. Rossing, *The Rapture Exposed: The Message of Hope in the Book of Revelation* (New York: Basic Books, 2004), Kindle edition, 25.

29 Ibid., 26.

30 Ibid., 25.

31 Ibid., 26.

32 Ibid., 26–27.

33 Cyrus I. Scofield, *Addresses on Prophecy* (Arno C. Gaebelein Press, n.d.), 26.

34 Wills, *Head and Heart*, 367.

35 Ibid.

CHAPTER EIGHT: GOD'S MISSION ACCORDING TO AMERICA

1 George M. Marsden, *Understanding Fundamentalism and Evangelicalism* (Grand Rapids, MI: Eerdmans, 1991), Kindle edition, 27.

2 George M. Marsden, *Fundamentalism and American Culture* (New York: Oxford University Press, 2006), 54–55.

3 Marsden, *Understanding Fundamentalism and Evangelicalism*, 29.

4 Garry Wills, *Head and Heart: A History of Christianity in America* (New York: Penguin, 2007), Kindle edition, location 5669.

5 Walter Rauschenbusch, *Christianity and the Social Crisis* (1907), 65–66.

6 Russell H. Conwell, "Acres of Diamonds" (1890), 23.

7 Frank Lambert, *Religion in American Politics: A Short History* (Princeton, NJ: Princeton University Press, 2008), Kindle edition, locations 1388–91.

8   " 'Bah!' Says Billy Sunday; 'My Critics? They'll Get Theirs,'
    Evangelist Asserts," *New York Times*, January 5, 1915, http:/
    /query.nytimes.com/mem/archive-free/pdf?res=F40815FE3E5C
    13738DDDAC0894D9405B858DF1D3.

9   *Brewers Journal*, vol. 38 (April 1912), 206.

10 Wills, *Head and Heart*, 410.

11 *New York Times*, January 5, 1915.

12 *National Bulletin*, vol. 5 (1913), 299.

13 Ibid., 298.

14 Washington Gladden, *Working People and Their Employers*
    (1885), 190.

15 Dr. Sider is also the author of the best-selling *Rich Christians in
    an Age of Hunger*, published in 1977.

16 Maggie Canty-Shafer, "Social Justice vs. Evangelism," *Relevant*,
    July 6, 2011, http://www.relevantmagazine.com/god/mission/fea
    tures/26115-social-justice-vs-evangelism.

17 Lambert, *Religion in American Politics*, locations 1480–83.

18 Stephen Prothero, *American Jesus: How the Son of God Became
    a National Icon* (New York: Farrar, Straus and Giroux, 2003),
    Kindle edition, 96.

19 Acts 1:8 (King James Version).

20 Wills, *Head and Heart*, 391.

21 Marsden, *Understanding Fundamentalism and Evangelicalism*,
    19.

22 Ibid., 20.

23 Josiah Strong, *Our Country: Its Possible Future and Its Present
    Crisis* (1891), 224.

24 Wills, *Head and Heart*, 393.

25 William Blum, *Killing Hope: U.S. Military and CIA Interventions
    Since World War II* (Montreal: Black Rose, 2000), 39.

26 Stuart Creighton Miller, *Benevolent Assimilation: The American
    Conquest of the Philippines, 1899–1903* (New Haven, CT: Yale
    University Press, 1982), 129.

27 Warren Zimmerman, *First Great Triumph: How Five Americans
    Made Their Country a World Power* (New York: Farrar, Straus

and Giroux, 2002), 351.

28 Mark A. Noll, *A History of Christianity in the United States and Canada* (Grand Rapids, MI: Eerdmans, 1992), Kindle edition, location 5095.

29 Wills, *Head and Heart*, 411.

30 Noll, *A History of Christianity in the United States and Canada*, locations 5095–97.

31 "Our Fight for the Heritage of Humanity; A Sermon," http://archive.org/stream/ourfightforherit00bart/ourfightforherit00bart_djvu.txt.

32 Ibid.

33 Lyman Abbott, *Inspiration for Daily Living: Selections from the Writings of Lyman Abbott* (1919), 95.

34 Lyman Abbott, *The Twentieth Century Crusade* (1918), 62.

35 Wills, *Head and Heart*, 412.

36 Ibid.

37 Ibid., 413.

38 Ibid., 420.

39 Brian Urquhart, "What You Can Learn from Reinhold Niebuhr," *New York Review of Books*, March 26, 2009, http://www.nybooks.com/articles/archives/2009/mar/26/what-you-can-learn-from-reinhold-niebuhr/?pagination=false.

40 Noll, *A History of Christianity in the United States and Canada*, locations 8615–17.

41 Reinhold Niebuhr, *The Irony of American History* (New York: Charles Scribner's Sons, 1952), 63.

42 Wills, *Head and Heart*, 454.

43 Lambert, *Religion in American Politics*, locations 2164–66.

44 David Brooks, "Obama, Gospel and Verse," *New York Times*, April 26, 2007, http://www.nytimes.com/2007/04/26/opinion/26brooks.html.

45 Reinhold Niebuhr, *Theologian of Public Life* (Minneapolis: Fortress Press, 1991), 127.

CHAPTER NINE: HOLY AMERICAN SPIRIT!

1   Mark A. Noll, *A History of Christianity in the United States and Canada* (Grand Rapids, MI: Eerdmans, 1992), Kindle edition, location 6339.

2   Richard J. Foster, *Streams of Living Water: Celebrating the Great Traditions of Christ* (New York: HarperCollins, 2010), 393.

3   Noll, *A History of Christianity in the United States and Canada*, location 6346.

4   Frank Bartleman, *Frank Bartleman's Azusa Street: First Hand Accounts of the Revival—Includes Feature Articles from the Apostolic Faith Newspaper* (Shippensburg, PA: Destiny Image, 2006), Kindle edition, location 64.

5   Ibid., locations 58–61.

6   Ibid., locations 386–89.

7   Ibid., locations 1082–83.

8   Ibid., location 920.

9   Ibid., location 836.

10 Ibid., locations 1134–35.

11 Ibid., locations 1173–77.

12 Harold Bloom, *The American Religion: The Emergence of the Post-Christian Nation* (New York: Simon & Schuster, 1993), 173.

13 Ibid., 171.

14 Douglas Sweeney, *The American Evangelical Story: A History of the Movement* (Grand Rapids, MI: Baker Academic, 2005), Kindle edition, 148.

15 Ibid., 149.

16 David L. Kimbrough, *Taking Up Serpents: Snake Handlers of Eastern Kentucky* (Macon, GA: Mercer University Press, 2002), 40.

17 Ibid., 133.

18 Stephen Prothero, *American Jesus: How the Son of God Became a National Icon* (New York: Farrar, Straus and Giroux, 2003), Kindle edition, 113.

19 Matthew Avery Sutton, *Aimee Semple McPherson and the Resurrection of Christian America* (Cambridge, MA: Harvard Univer-

sity Press, 2007), 2.

20 Ibid.

21 Ibid.

22 Ibid., 1–3.

23 Ibid., 3.

24 Daniel Mark Epstein, *Sister Aimee: The Life of Aimee Semple McPherson* (San Diego: Harvest, 1993), 295.

25 Milton Berle, *Milton Berle: An Autobiography by Milton Berle* (Milwaukee: Applause, 2002), 129.

26 Kate Bowler, *Blessed: A History of the American Prosperity Gospel* (New York: Oxford University Press, 2013), Kindle edition, locations 77–78.

27 Ibid., locations 78–80.

28 Ibid., location 311.

29 Ibid., location 297.

30 Ibid., locations 783–85.

31 Ibid., locations 1485–86.

32 Jesse Duplantis, "When Will We Yield to the Anointing of Wealth II," April 10, 2005, quoted at "Jesse Duplantis—False Preacher /Teachings," Forgotten Word Ministries, http://www.forgotten-word.org/duplantis.html.

33 "Leroy Thompson—Money Cometh to Me Now!!," YouTube, http://www.youtube.com/watch?v=8oXhYVm2MW8.

34 Leonardo Blair, "'Preachers of LA' Trailer Teases with Lavish, Dramatic Lifestyles of Six Mega-Pastors," *Christian Post*, June 28, 2013, http://www.christianpost.com/news/preachers-of-la-trailer-teases-with-lavish-dramatic-lifestyles-of-six-mega-pastors-99070/.

35 Ibid.

36 http://www.youtube.com/watch?v=2becyRCK6LU#t=28.

CHAPTER TEN: ONE NATION UNDER GODS

1 George M. Marsden, *Understanding Fundamentalism and Evangelicalism* (Grand Rapids, MI: Eerdmans, 1991), Kindle edition, 4.

2 Kevin Roose, *The Unlikely Disciple: A Sinner's Semester at Amer-*

ica's Holiest University (New York: Grand Central, 2009), Kindle edition, location 4953.

3   Susan Friend Harding, *The Book of Jerry Falwell: Fundamentalist Language and Politics* (Princeton, NJ: Princeton University Press, 2000), 154.

4   Ibid., 126.

5   Ibid.

6   Ibid.

7   Garry Wills, *Head and Heart: A History of Christianity in America* (New York: Penguin Press, 2007), Kindle edition, 491.

8   Sydney E. Ahlstrom, "Theology and the Present-Day Revival," *Annals of the American Academy of Political and Social Science*, November 1960.

9   Roger Bruns, *Billy Graham: A Biography* (Westport, CT: Greenwood Press, 2004), 24.

10 David Aikman, *Billy Graham: His Life and Influence* (Nashville: Thomas Nelson, 2007), 37.

11 "Billy Graham," Biography.com, http://www.biography.com/people/billy-graham-9317669?page=2.

12 Angela M. Lahr, *Millennial Dreams and Apocalyptic Nightmares: The Cold War Origins of Political Evangelism* (New York: Oxford University Press, 2007), 3.

13 Ibid., 116.

14 Andrew Himes, *The Sword of the Lord: The Roots of Fundamentalism in an American Family* (Seattle: Chiara Press, 2011), Kindle edition, locations 4806–7.

15 Ibid., location 5194.

16 Ibid., location 5197.

17 Ibid., locations 5201–6.

18 Carl F. H. Henry, *The Uneasy Conscience of Modern Fundamentalism* (Grand Rapids, MI: Eerdmans, 1947), 2.

19 Ibid., 18.

20 Himes, *The Sword of the Lord*, location 5213.

21 Ibid., locations 5223–25.

22 Ibid., locations 5234–36.

23 Curtis Hutson, *New Evangelicalism: An Enemy of Fundamentalism* (Murfreesboro, TN: Sword of the Lord, 1984), 16.

24 Jon Meacham, "Pilgrim's Progress," *Newsweek*, August 13, 2006.

25 "Public Opinion and the Vietnam War," Digital History, http://www.digitalhistory.uh.edu/active_learning/explorations/vietnam/vietnam_pubopinion.cfm.

26 *The Public Papers of the Presidents of the United States: William J. Clinton, 2000,* 799.

27 Julia Kirk Blackwelder, "Southern White Fundamentalists and the Civil Rights Movement," *Phylon* 40, no. 4 (4th quarter 1979): 334–41.

28 L. Calvin Bacon, "Eyewitness at a Funeral," *The Pentecostal Evangel* (July 14, 1968), 20–21.

29 Ibid.

30 "Billy Graham and Civil Rights," Learn NC, http://www.learnnc.org/lp/editions/nchist-postwar/6121.

31 Wills, *Head and Heart,* 470.

32 Michael Lienesch, *Redeeming America: Piety and Politics in the New Christian Right* (Chapel Hill: University of North Carolina Press, 1993), 82.

33 Wills, *Head and Heart,* 485.

34 Ibid.

35 Ibid., 491–92.

36 Ibid.

37 Martha F. Lee, *Conspiracy Rising: Conspiracy Thinking and American Public Life* (Santa Barbara, CA: Praeger, 2011), 92.

38 Wills, *Head and Heart,* 494.

39 Daniel Williams, *God's Own Party: The Making of the Christian Right* (New York: Oxford University Press, 2010), Kindle edition, 250.

40 Ibid., 255.

41 Ibid.

42 Ibid.

43 Wills, *Head and Heart,* 512.

44 Ibid.

45 Williams, *God's Own Party*, 268.

46 Katie Barge and Nicole Casta, "Self-Proclaimed 'Missionary to the Media' Falwell Made 12th Appearance Since Election," Media Matters, December 6, 2004, http://mediamatters.org /research/2004/12/06/self-proclaimed-missionary-to-the-media -falwell/132400.

47 "Rick Warren's Inaugural Invocation," *Christianity Today*, January 20, 2009, http://blog.christianitytoday.com/ctpolitics/2009/ 01/rick_warrens_in.html.